Ford Farewell Mills and Gatsch

Stagings

Foreword by
Michael Farewell

Introduction by
Susan Doubilet

Photographic Credits

Otto Baitz / Esto: 13, 15, 17, 47, 64
Chuck Choi: 39, 40, 41, 42, 43, 55, 56, 57, 59, 109, 110, 112, 113, 121, 122, 123
Thaddeus DuBois Govan, Jr.: 87, 88, 89, 91
Alison Harris: 135
Christopher Lovi: 99, 100, 101, 102, 103
Martin Photography Inc.: cover
Michael Moran: 16
Brian Rose: 19, 21, 31, 32, 37, 48, 49, 51, 53, 67, 68, 69, 71, 72, 73, 94, 95 (top)
Taylor Photo: frontispiece, 23, 24, 25, 28, 29, 33, 36, 61, 65, 75, 76, 77, 81, 82-83, 84, 85, 93, 95 (bottom), 105, 106, 107, 125, 129, 131, 132, 133, 134

Special thanks to Alison Harris and Meredith Arms Bzdak for their editorial guidance.

Chief Editor of Collection
Maurizio Vitta

Publishing Coordinator
Franca Rottola

Editorial Staff
Cristina Rota

Graphic Design
Marco Maulucci

Editing and Translation
Aaron Maines

Colour-separation
Chromia, Meda, Milano

Printing
Bolis Poligrafiche Bergamo

First Published
October 2001

Copyright 2001
by l'Arca Edizioni

All rights reserved
Printed in Italy

ISBN 88-7838-090-3

Contents

5	Introduction by *Susan Doubilet*
9	Foreword by *Michael Farewell*
11	*Brick Works*
12	Crescent Houses at The Lawrenceville School, Lawrenceville, NJ
18	Bainbridge House, Princeton, NJ
22	Civic Square I: Center for the Arts and Planning at Rutgers University, New Brunswick, NJ
30	New Jersey Historical Society, Newark, NJ
38	F.M. Kirby Shakespeare Theatre at Drew University, Madison, NJ
45	*Stone Works*
46	Legislative Chambers and Addition to the New Jersey State House, Trenton, NJ
54	Pool, Pool House and Landscape II, Fisher's Island, NY
60	Princeton University Graduate College, Princeton, NJ
66	Somerset County Courthouse, Somerville, NJ
74	Civic Square III: Middlesex County Courthouse, New Brunswick, NJ
79	*Wood Works*
80	Princeton Child Development Institute, Lawrence Township, NJ
86	New Jersey Housing & Mortgage Finance Agency, Trenton, NJ
92	University Cottage Club Library, Princeton, NJ
97	*Stucco Works*
98	Pool and Pool House I, Far Hills, NJ
104	Casino Building at Georgian Court College, Lakewood, NJ
108	Far Hills Country Day School, Far Hills, NJ
114	South Orange Arts Center, South Orange, NJ
119	*Steel Works*
120	Department of Art and Archaeology at Princeton University, Princeton, NJ
124	Cityscape Center Master Plan, New Brunswick, NJ
130	From the Lighthouse, Atlantic City, NJ
137	Credits
142	Firm History
143	List of Employees

Introduction
by Susan Doubilet

FFMG: The Duality of Design and Preservation

The Princeton architectural firm of Ford Farewell Mills and Gatsch is as professional as its imposing name implies. But as its work proves, it also exhibits a deep yearning for spiritual connection. The buildings – preserved or newly built - impart a sense of rightness and of calm, reassuring to those who use them and, at the same time, quietly inspiring.

The key to this calm might lie in the dual nature of the office - the firm is nationally known for its high-level preservation work led by partner Michael Mills, and for its innovative new design, now guided by Michael Farewell - and it is worth exploring to what extent the coexistence of the two departments affects the results. The expectations aroused are threefold: that preservation's concentration on the material aspects of building is an excellent basic training for all the architects in the firm; that the boldness and awareness that new design requires of architects broadens the horizons of preservationists; and that both sets of professionals share an intense interest in the spiritual qualities of architecture.

The Materials of Building

As to the material nature of architecture, the first clue to the firm's focus on this aspect lies in the organization of this monograph itself. The buildings are presented by material type – stone, wood, and so on – signaling that for these professionals, architecture is not merely an intellectual exercise propped up by the specifications of engineers, but one in which function, stability, and aesthetics are completely interwoven with the materials both seen and unseen.

The proof of the theory is in the buildings, of course, and we can examine several examples in the oeuvre. The Pool House on Fishers Island (p. 54) can be described simply as retaining walls and a roof, but what retaining walls, and what a roof. Massive stones make up the earth-hugging walls of the pool and cabana, suggesting a grotto of hidden pleasures and forming a forceful connection to the land. The roof, on the other hand, is a thin sheet of fabric stretched like a kite over an aluminum and wood frame. Where the stone conveys stability, the roof communicates lightness and stimulates one to soar – up and into the pool, up and beyond one's fantasies. While the sun lingers lovingly over the stone wall's every crevice and craggy spot, it moves quickly around and through the stretched fabric, causing it to glow.

A more literal (and at the same time playful) demonstration of the qualities of different materials occurs in the new headquarters for New Jersey Housing and Mortgage Finance Agency (p. 86). The architects renovated a former cable testing laboratory in the Roebling Industrial Complex in Trenton, and in the interior created four squares dominated by little "buildings," each of a different material and each representing a separate department of the agency. The executive branch of the institution – its solid core – is represented by a circular structure of ground-faced concrete masonry units. Homebuyers sign their mortgage papers in a light-filled wood lath cube topped by wood trusses. The no-nonsense administrative wing has a simple structure of steel, laid out in a grid inspired by Mondrian, and is faced with a wall of window units, repetitive like punched cards. And the financial branch's aedicule looks like the traditional bank, with a colonnaded, stuccoed facade. Those using the headquarters, all involved in one form or another in the world of buildings, cannot help but be pleasantly diverted and inadvertently instructed in the variety available in construction materials.

The Far Hills Country Day School addition (p. 108) represents a new level of technological expression endeavored, if not quite attained, by these architects. The west facade of the building, which faces an outdoor amphitheater, appears to be a "thin" wall of metal panels, shaded by metal louvers, in contrast to the sturdy concrete block walls of the remaining facades. In fact, budget constraints did not allow for the panels, and instead, stucco, scored to mimic panels, was used over concrete block to achieve the intended visual effect. To complete the artful fakery, the non-adjustable horizontal louvers scarcely protect the wall from strong sunlight. But it is a very pretty look and a preparation, perhaps, for the firm's future realization of the intended wall type.

The everyday practice of preservation architecture can serve as the most extensive and intensive course of study possible on the uses and detailing of appropriately (and, sometimes, inappropriately) selected materials. In the restoration of the Essex Club (now the New Jersey Historical Society, p. 30) in Newark, the architects had to develop methods to repair and replace severely damaged limestone. In the interior, walnut paneling had to be conserved and the finish restored. The 1765 Bainbridge House in Princeton (p. 18) presented a challenge pervasive in the restoration of buildings: the incorporation of state-of-the-art climate control systems and structural reinforcement without disturbance to the historic building fabric. Exemplifying the nimble thinking required of preservationists is the barrier-free access device used here: the historical wooden yard fence was reconstructed and adapted for the purpose. In the restoration of the exemplary Graduate College at Princeton University (p. 60), designed by Ralph Adams Cram in 1911, the woodwork, plaster, stone, and metals had to be carefully repaired or restored. The 1909 Somerset County Courthouse (p. 66) called for cleaning, repairing, structural bracing, and replacing marble walls and parapet, windows and roof. In addition, the architects carried out research into the original finish of the design's focal point, the cupola, and installed, as a result, a new flat seam copper roof. Such examples of intensive knowledge and experience with materials can be listed almost indefinitely, it seems, in the work of this one firm, but the subject cannot be left without mention of the restoration of the New Jersey State House (p. 46), an amalgam of buildings constructed over the course of two hundred years. While compliance with the existing building code and the integration of up-to-date mechanical and electrical systems undoubtedly presented an enormous challenge, the restoration and re-creation of a vast panoply of historic finishes in the General Assembly and Senate Chambers offered the most dramatic results. Following research conducted by the preservationists, expert craftsman were called in and directed in the recreation of decorative plaster work, scagliola, gold leaf, stained glass, murals, brass light fixtures, and millwork with exuberant effects, uncannily recreating the Gesamtkunstwerk of former times.

Do the two sets of experience, from preservation work and new design, influence each other? The architects themselves feel too close to the situation to answer definitively on the subject, but the likelihood is that they do. The evidence of the new design demonstrates that the architects do not merely repeat a set of details in a limited number of material choices, but that they are open to many options, depending on the specific project and the cultural messages they want to convey. And their confident approach to materials undoubtedly contributes to the calmness that their designs exude.

Design, Preservation, and Contextualism

How does new design affect preservation work? Design, as mentioned in the first paragraphs of this essay, requires on the one hand courage to express one's own creative opinions, and on the other hand an awareness of the contemporary culture for inspiration and substance. Unfortunately, preservationists all too often fall back on reproduction to bring about what they call contextual harmony when called upon to restructure our built environment, in making additions to existing structures, for example. This is clearly not the case in the work of this firm, and a number of examples are at hand.

The Pool House on Fishers Island serves, here again, as an outstanding illustration of how an addition can be tied to its context and yet still have its own individual expression. The pool extends the rugged granite foundation walls of the picturesque 1930s house on the site. Like the house, the pool house seems to grow from the landscape. And like it, as well, it combines whimsy with naturalism. But unlike the house, it is abstract in form. And unlike it, it opens out toward infinity – the seemingly boundless ocean and the heavens above. Among his architectural heroes Farewell points to the modern Italian master Carlo Scarpa who, he says, "always stands as a model for the highly deliberate engagement of a new order with historical artifacts." In fact, it is a hero of Scarpa's, namely Frank Lloyd Wright, that comes more immediately to mind as one regards the Fishers Island project. Not as encrusted with symbolic details as Scarpa's works, it seems to penetrate the earth and emerge with earth's stony component in a manner that owes homage to Fallingwater. Also reminiscent of that iconic residence is the pool house's paradoxical ability simultaneously to burrow and to soar.

Another pool house designed by the firm for a suburban site (p. 98) makes a statement about its context. The design seems to take an anti-contextual stance. This project is both chunky and symmetrical, in complete contrast to the client's ranch house on the property. But what does the suburban context consist of other than a collection of single-family houses of various styles posing on their large sites? Furthermore, if we extend the idea of "context" to include "historical context," we can see this small design as representative of the post-postmodern era. The architects have reached down into the bag of historical forms and – brushing past classicism, historical romanticism, modernism and postmodernism – pulled out a primitive-cum-modern pattern of their own device, not unlike the sturdy forms of the American modernist Louis Kahn. As to the context of the landscape itself, Farewell claims to place his buildings within nature in a manner influenced by his former employer, Michael Graves. Though Farewell's buildings are more abstract than Graves's classically-inspired ones, their modest position within the landscape – as if they were joyful elements on a par with stands of trees, bushes, and knolls – are indeed reminiscent of the work of Farewell's mentor.

The Far Hills Country Day School addition is an intelligent and stylish response to the matter of contextualism. The new addition is as smart as the pre-existing structure is bland, and yet the new wing does not talk down to the old. Like the old wing, the addition employs concrete block as the major exterior material. At the same time, the two-story height of the new classroom wing provides a vertical counterpoint to the older one-story wing, and the horizontal louvers offer a crispness that the old building lacks.

The addition of an office wing to the New Jersey State House presented quite a different challenge. Rather than lacking personality, in this case the pre-existing complex had, one might say, too much personality. Expanded frequently between the late 18th century and the late 20th century, the State House reflects numerous periods of architectural history. The stylistic choice for the addition was appropriate in its simplicity and near-neutrality in contrast to the fancy-dress ball represented by the older buildings. An almost unornamented two-story granite-clad structure with simple punched windows, the new office wing nonetheless implies Classical antecedents with its regular rhythms and barely perceptible pilasters.
The idea of setting the structure up as a "unifying base" to the existing buildings sounds clever, and for this purpose it has a fittingly sturdy appearance, but it does tend to distort the proportions of the historic structures from the south side. Still, it provides a ceremonial entrance lobby for the Legislative branch, and links the complex to the newly restored waterfront park.

Once again, then, the existence of two equally strong departments within one architecture firm proves to be a decided advantage. Additions by the firm provide a graceful bridge between historic buildings and the contemporary environment, and at the same time are strong and distinctive creations in their own right.

Spiritualism and Symbolism in Architecture

This brings us to the final expectation of the preservation/new design firm, that is, the anticipation that its two halves would value equally, and with a sense of historical perspective, the spiritual quality of architecture. In preservation, one can look to the restored lavishness of the State House, the restrained gothic richness of Princeton's Graduate Center, and the simplicity of the Bainbridge House to see how totally the architects have entered into the spirit of each individual time and place. In new design, it is fruitful to look once more at the exemplary Pool House on Fishers Island, a relatively small structure that connects on so many levels to the spirit of the place and program as broadly and imaginatively defined.

As mentioned above, the pool house's granite walls are related materially and spiritually to the earth, while the sail-like roof refers to distant ships and airplanes visible from the site. The one evokes feelings of heaviness and vacation languor, the other, of the lightness of flight. And behind the earth/sky imagery are two mythological stories that the architects claim as inspiration for the design: the story of Theseus fleeing the labyrinth, and the tale of Daedalus and Icarus taking flight on wax wings. In another reference to mythological figures, the pool floor is inlaid with a map of the constellations.

The gently curved roof appears not only on the Fishers Island pool house but also on a great many of the firm's new structures. It seems to evoke, however, different feelings in the various applications. On Fishers Island, as discussed, it creates a sensation of lightness and provides inspiration for movement and change. On the Far Hills country Day School, the curved roof spans over the stairhall/commons area as well as over the new classrooms. Here, the impressions are of vastness and at the same time unity. In the Princeton Child Development Institute, and in many other of the firm's residential buildings, the curved roofs seem protective, even maternal, offering reassurance and comfort – in a word, shelter.

Shelter

In the final analysis, then, the work of FFMG seems to meet the expectations engendered by its preservation/new design duality. Preservation's involvement in a wide variety of materials spills over in the work of the new-design architects. The preservationists' interest in contextualism is heeded by the new-design people, who respond in their own creative and contemporary ways. And both groups are dedicated to the spirit and symbolism of design.

And how do these qualities produce the sense of rightness and calm observed overall in the firm's design? The answer is in the concept of shelter. The instinct of these architects is first to reassure those who come in contact with their buildings, thereby giving them the courage to enter the world's stage, and thus inspiring them to act out their potential.

Foreword
by Michael Farewell

This body of work, the product of a fifteen year span, is grounded in the conviction that architecture is essentially theatre, that both restored historic spaces and expressive new places have the capability to intensify, heighten, and make memorable the rituals of use and occupation.
Like theatre, this work draws deeply on remembrance and tradition while expressing the immediacy of the present moment. It is work that provides a stage for the human figure, a dramatization of the everyday and the familiar. It is a heightening of the real, and at moments, it is almost dreamlike in its suggestion of human activity. Because this is work that addresses both cultural resources and the immediacy of the contemporary, historic preservation and new architecture move through these pages like two dancers. At times, in specific projects, the two figures move in close proximity and reciprocal movement. At other times, one or the other discipline acts solely, although its partner is never further than the wings of the stage. This dance of the old and new has been the recurrent theme of the work, and, perhaps not surprisingly, it culminates in the recent focus in the practice on actual theatres and performing arts centers – engaging both historic buildings and new spaces.

This period begins with the seminal project of the New Jersey State House restoration and addition. Encompassing both the comprehensive preservation of the legislative chambers and other notable parts of the capitol from various historic periods, the project entailed the carefully coordinated installation of new mechanical, electrical and plumbing systems in meticulously restored historic spaces. Based on historic research, light fixtures were reconditioned, *scagliola* columns were recreated and repaired, and murals were cleaned and newly lighted. All of this work was done to provide the expressive setting for the high theatre of the political process. The act of governing is given a revitalized setting which draws deeply on historic tradition. The juxtaposition of contemporary figures against the historical background situates the political process in a layered, referential context.

Pure preservation for such an intense public use requires a great deal of support program accommodation. To reduce the population density in the building and to provide a new entry from the south side of the complex, an office addition was built. This two-story block is configured as a stylobate or base for the neoclassical State House above and behind it, in much the same way that the Adelphi terrace on the Thames supports Somerset House. The sculpted granite base, with battered corners and a carved character to the interior detailing, provides the platform for the lighter, more delicate historical forms above. Thus, the new work provides a frame for viewing the original building, a reading reinforced in the new south lobby where the south portico is literally framed in a skylight view.

Immediately after the design of the State House project, the potential for developing a building/stage was further explored in Pool House I. Based on the simple idea of framing a swimmer about to enter the water, the structure is pared down to a single proscenium constructed of elemental materials of integral color stucco, natural fir plank, and bluestone paving. The excavated volume of the pool corresponds to the volume of the pool house; the two volumes are reciprocal, and both are occupiable. With the minimal program requirements housed in the wings, the central aperture is open to the landscape beyond, and the fugitive effects of light and shadow are recorded in this empty space.

Just as Pool House I represents a reduction of architectural vocabulary after the multi-layered complexities of the New Jersey State House, the Bainbridge House restoration provided a more pure eighteenth century context for preservation. Now used as a museum, the adaptive use of the house entailed accessibility improvements, discrete insertion of museum quality systems, structural enhancements, and the painstaking restoration of historic materials. The eighteenth century building is both a container of gallery shows and an exhibit in its own right. The drama here resides in juxtapositions: of museum program with historic house, of modern figures with eighteenth-century rooms. The museum, inherently a framer of archival material and historical artifacts, is here given a participatory role in the collection, and the role of the viewer is brought into critical play.

These preoccupations with history and framing devices led to Pool House II on Fishers Island, a setting for the exploration of both disciplines. A 1930s house set on the north shore of the island was somewhat detached from its overgrown landscape. Through extension of the granite walls of the basement out into a nearby ravine and reshaping of the landscape, a new stage-like space was created. This platform, framed on two sides by labyrinth-like enclosing walls, recalls ruins and sacred sites. The human figure and the landscape are here framed by a variety of openings and apertures. The original house, restored and connected to the new garden structure, dynamically engages the undulating topography and the Sound beyond. The rustic, natural house is sharply focused by contrast with a wing-like structure, highly machined, tensile, and cantilevered. Like the ships and planes that dart through this nineteenth century landscape, this new structure connects the historical place to a contemporary world. Importantly, the viewer is given a place to stand to survey this spectacle.

It is in institutions that this potential for a dialogue of new and old, and the intersection of use and architecture becomes especially charged. At the Department of Art and Archaeology at Princeton University, issues of identity and materiality become the subject of the work. The renovation of three floors of McCormick Hall provided an opportunity to create a new identity for the teaching spaces and administrative offices. In a kind of architectural discourse on art historical analysis, the plan is configured as a diptych, with a centralized, carved space in one panel and an open plan, screened space in the other. These two worlds are juxtaposed and reveal the character of each other along the central spine of the space. In homage to art history's ubiquitous slide projector, a light fixture projects the image of the dual plan onto the floor of the gallery. This phantom image is contrasted with a plaster cast of an Eleusian initiation scene that terminates the main axis. Thus the art historians move in a physical space that echoes the deeper programmatic agenda.

The emphasis on materiality and the complex intersection of building systems extends to the Somerset Courthouse, a 1920s marble structure suffering from extensive material degradation. In addition to exterior restoration and repair, the interior of this refined county courthouse was repainted in original colors discovered through historic paint analysis. This highly detailed setting is given ceremonial dignity through restoration of its original character. The preservationist is like an archaeologist, revealing deeper layers of historical form and ushering them back to the surface. There are rooms and spaces that exude an aura of an historical moment, and embody an attitude towards justice and the public realm.

The capability of modernist space to express this ritualized aspect of public life is the intention behind the addition to the Far Hills Country Day School. Here the idea of a place of public assembly, a central meeting space configured as an amphitheatre, is carried into both landscape and building so that the two are welded together. This upper school wing, comprising six classrooms and support spaces, is constructed of the same concrete block as the original structure. In sharp contrast, a stucco plane with an aluminum louver system lightens the wall into a scrim, and replaces a hard envelope with a porous screen. The building is an exploration of different characters of natural light, all in support of human interactions in different groupings. Spare and elemental, the building is a backdrop or setting for the life of student and teacher.

Many of these themes of identity and form, memory and framing culminate in the project for the New Jersey Shakespeare Festival. Here preservation of a 1908 gymnasium building and addition and adaptation for use as a theatre focused the subject of the dialogue of old and new. Since the Festival's mission is the contemporary production of classic plays, the theme of original and contemporary is at the heart of its work. The building sets out to evoke this character. Through reorientation of the building front, and creation of an exterior stage-like space, the audience becomes actor and participant in this drama. Terraces, elevated platforms and balconies are the field for enacting this life of the theatre. The original facade, stripped of windows, becomes a portal to the

house. The house itself fuses theatrical apparatus and machinery with the fragmented enclosing walls of the original building. One has a sense of tradition confronting the immediacy of the present, of memory and experience in sharp and poignant adjacency.

If the theatre interior represents the focused development of these themes, the urban setting represents its broadening. As Christine Boyer prescribes in *The City of Collective Memory*, "The public realm of the City of Collective Memory should entail a continuous urban topography, a spatial structure that covers both rich and poor places, honorific and humble monuments, permanent and ephemeral forms, and should include places for public assemblage and public debate, as well as private memory walks and personal retreats." Urban design, and design of urban buildings, is inherently concerned with cultural continuity and the incorporation of historical form into new environments. The memory theatre and the place of public appearance is the urban essence.

The New Brunswick Cityscape plan, along with no fewer than seven building commissions, sets out to reinforce the fabric of this colonial era town and to extend its reinvention. A small city which has great vitality from its public university community, health care corporate headquarters, and theatre district, New Brunswick's fabric had been frayed by urban renewal and socio-economic changes. The Cityscape plan proposes major redevelopment which incorporates housing, corporate offices, theaters, commercial uses, a hotel conference center, and a college boathouse.

The strategy has been based on reinforcing pedestrian movement, defining streets, connecting programmed zones and achieving real urban density. The goal is the continued development of this small city as a place to live and visit, a rich urban spectacle in sharp contrast to suburban diffusion of uses. The specific projects related to this plan, courthouse and university, theatres and restored 18th century house, create just the sort of charged field or stage that merges memory with contemporary experience and allows the viewer to simultaneously occupy several worlds.

This book, in support of this thesis that these preservation projects and new design projects share a conviction about the built environment, is organized by materiality rather than program or discipline. Brick works include explorations in material restoration as well as expressions of the hand-laid scale of this material in new design; stucco's capabilities for crisp geometric surfaces as well as backdrops for shadows lead to coupling a pool house and a restored pleasure casino. At the heart of this presentation is the conviction that the fact of the material, its physical character and interaction with other materials, is a drama in itself.

Brick Works

Frederick Law Olmsted prepared the original design for The Lawrenceville School campus, a ring of houses around a circle, in 1886. Over the years the plan was extended and redefined with the introduction of new buildings, notably those designed by Delano & Aldrich, which were sited along an open-ended quadrangle in a grid plan. The 1985 decision by the school's Board of Trustees to admit girls led to further campus expansion; specifically, new residential facilities were required. This need for girls' dormitories provided the impetus to develop a new campus master plan that could reintegrate the campus. By siting the new dormitories in a crescent near the original circle, a new outdoor room was defined. The placement of the dormitories also provided a link to modern dining and athletic facilities, located at the periphery of the property, drawing them closer to the core of the campus.

These four dormitories draw on the original Circle Houses for inspiration, which in turn were based upon the English boarding school tradition of a house-based academic and social structure. The new, three-story houses, each with two faculty apartments and rooms for thirty-two students, are similar to one another but alternately reversed in plan. The buildings are zoned horizontally, with student spaces in the front and faculty apartments in the back, and vertically, with students' rooms on the upper levels and social activity rooms, lounge, parlor and television room, and support spaces at grade.

The intention of the design was to reinforce Olmsted's view of the interdependency of building and landscape. Thus, together with McGraw Infirmary, which was renovated and enlarged by the firm as part of the same project, the Crescent Houses are closely grouped behind an arc of 100 year-old oak and maple trees to form a screen-like boundary to this campus edge. The brick buildings are increasingly articulated toward the inside of the arc, with the front "crescent" facades bracketed and banded with contrasting brick. To further emphasize this articulation, projecting lounges change sequentially along the line of the arc. Large-scale gestures, such as the two-story bays, clustered windows, and projecting eaves relate in scale to the space of the crescent. The character of the materials, the detailing of the steel brackets and windows, and the aluminum roofs refer to both the original Peabody and Stearns Circle Houses and the steel and brick modernism of the 1970s dining hall nearby.

Lawrenceville, NJ, 1987

Crescent Houses at The Lawrenceville School

View of the dormitories.

Ground floor plan.

Second floor plan.

Third floor plan.

Site plan.

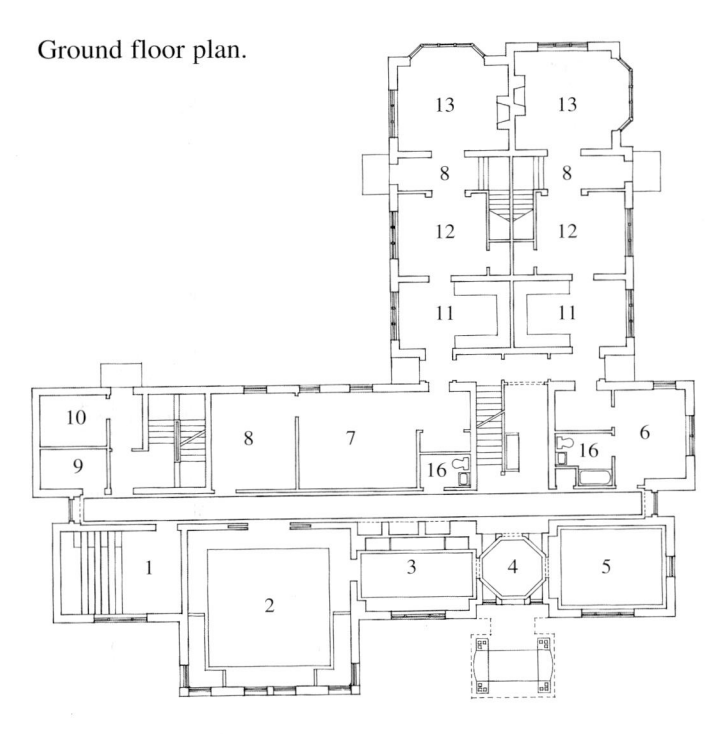

1. TV Room
2. Lounge
3. Coat Room
4. Foyer
5. Parlor
6. Residence Room
7. Family Room
8. Study
9. Vending Room
10. Trash Room
11. Kitchen
12. Dining Room
13. Living Room
14. Telephone Room
15. Custodial Closet
16. Bath Room
17. Bed Room

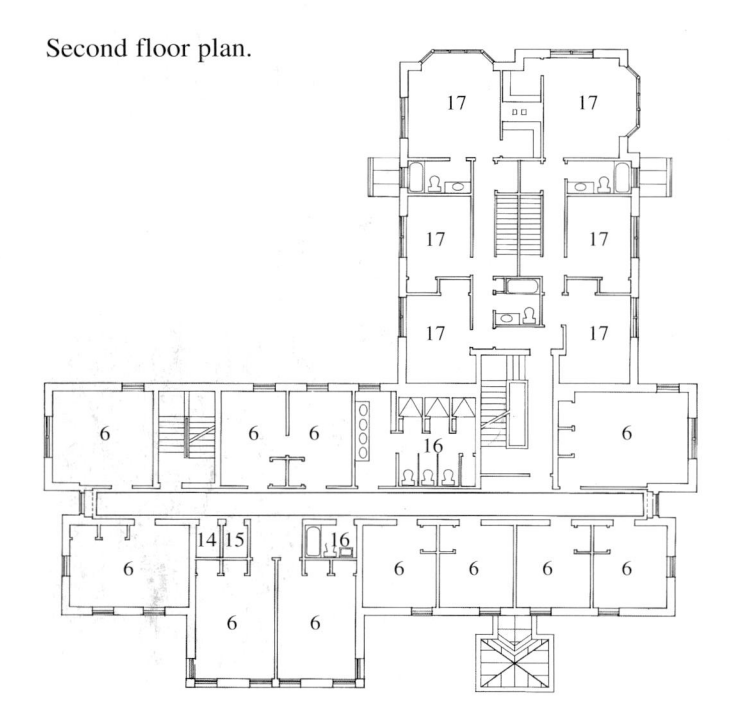

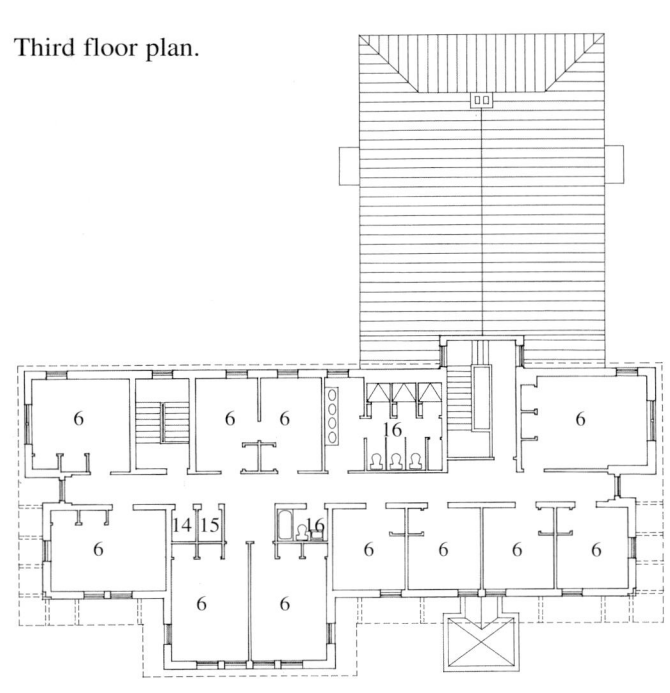

Elevation.

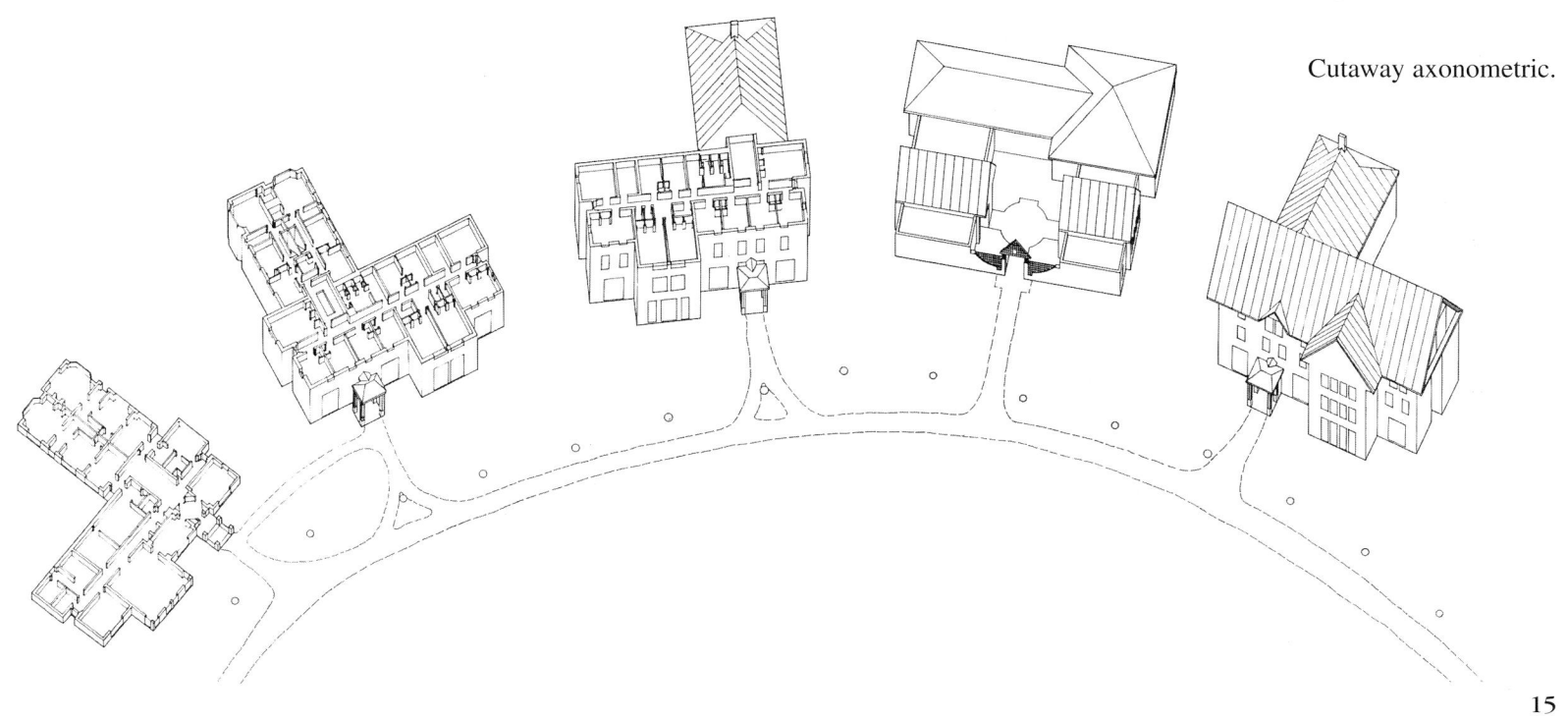

Cutaway axonometric.

15

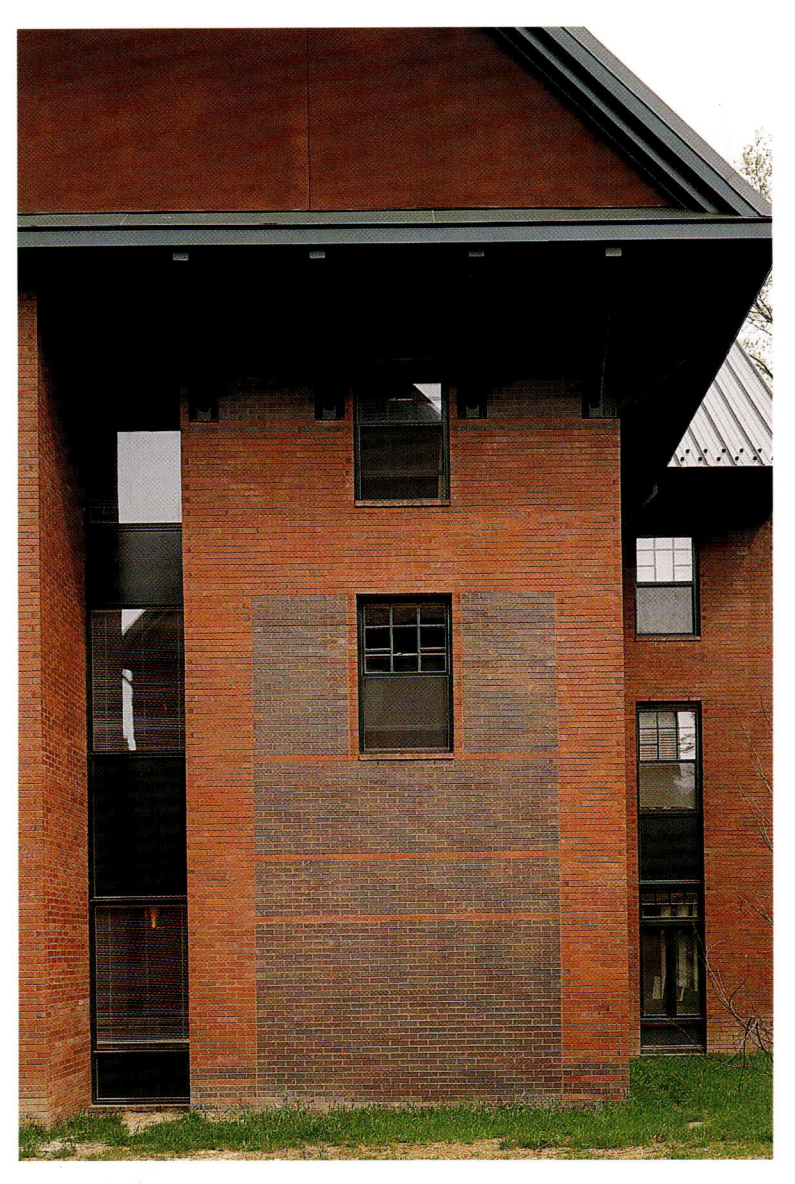

Detail view of north elevation.

Entry foyer.

Lounge.

Opposite, perspective view of the houses.

16

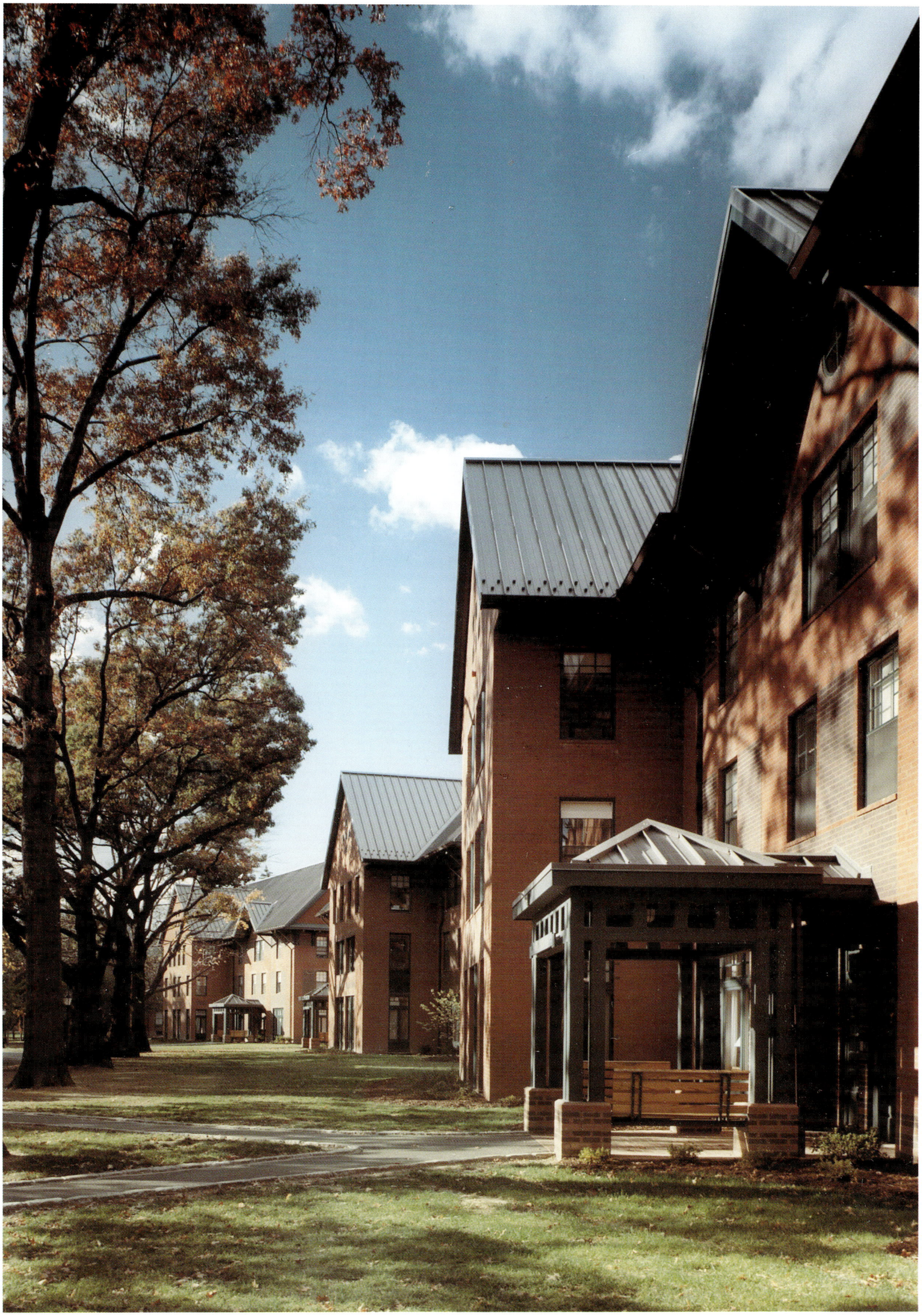

This circa 1765 house is operated as a historical museum, library, and archives for the Historical Society of Princeton. Originally the residence of Commodore Bainbridge in the eighteenth century, it was converted and used as a University dormitory in the nineteenth and early twentieth centuries, and then served as the Princeton Borough Library until 1964. The restoration of this building gave the Historical Society the unique opportunity to showcase an eighteenth-century structure, one of the last survivors of its era along Nassau Street, the borough's primary thoroughfare.

As with the majority of the firm's preservation projects, a plan for the preservation of Bainbridge House was completed prior to design development and used to guide the subsequent renovation and restoration activities. Major grants that provided funding to support the work were pursued and received from the National Endowment for the Humanities and the New Jersey Historic Trust.

The project required the addition of the technology necessary to operate a modern museum, while respecting the historic structure and finishes of the building. Structural reinforcements were made to meet current loading capacity requirements and to allow removal of unsightly lally columns that had been added when the house served as a library. Fire suppression systems were added to protect the building and collection and to improve life safety. A climate control system was designed to achieve museum conditions while being nearly invisible. Major systems of electrical conduit and piping were carefully located to avoid damage to historic fabric, and coordinated with HVAC and fire protection systems. The new programmable lighting system included recessed track lights, accent lights, and floor mounted outlets for the Historical Society's changing exhibits.

On the interior, finishes were reproduced based upon microscopic analysis of remaining original paints and glazes. The Historical Society presently uses the first floor for its more public functions, which include a series of changing exhibitions, more permanent period displays, and a shop. Its administrative offices, conference room, library, and archives occupy the second and third floors.

The reconstruction of a wooden yard fence, a historic feature that had been removed in the twentieth century, aided the effort to design barrier-free access that would be in keeping with the historical qualities of the facade.

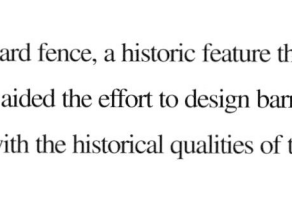

Princeton, NJ, 1992

Bainbridge House

South and west (front) elevations.

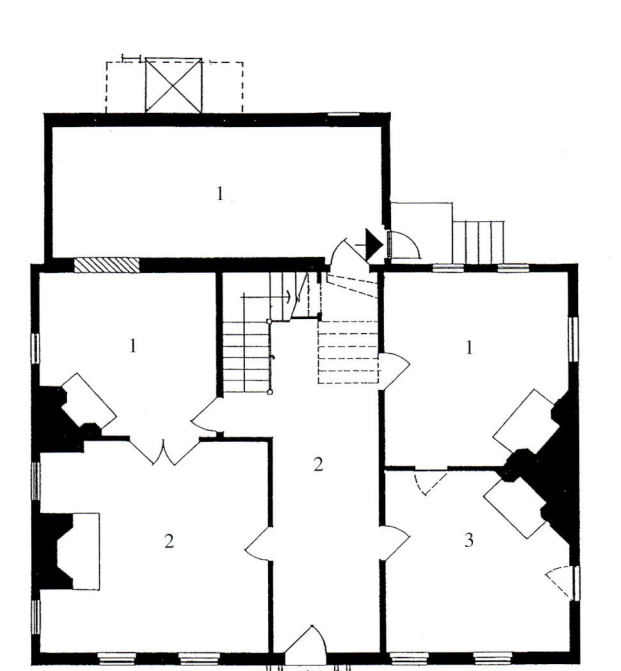

First floor plan.

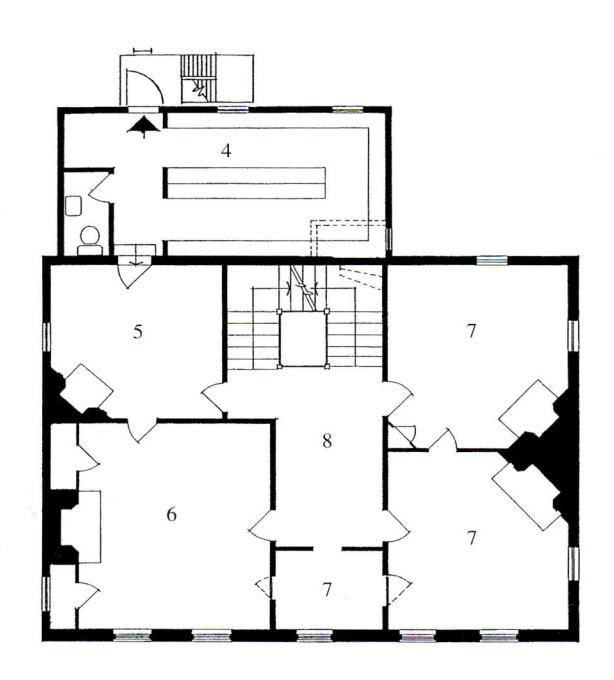

Second floor plan.

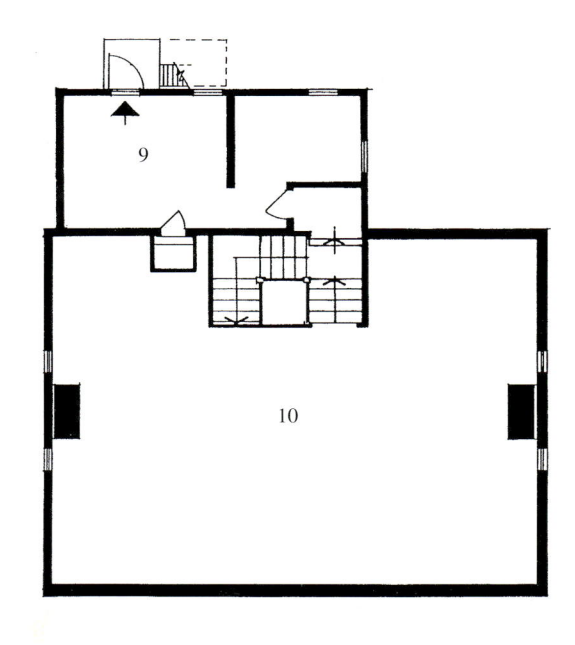

Third floor plan.

1. Exhibition
2. Period Room
3. Gift Shop
4. Library Stacks
5. Reading Room
6. Board Room
7. Office
8. Hall
9. Photo/Archive
10. Mechanical

Exhibition room.

Hall, first floor.

The new Center for the Arts and Planning, located on a major block in downtown New Brunswick that includes the State Theater, two other theaters, City Hall, a church and post office, represents a major commitment by New Jersey's State University to maintain its urban identity. The site is a gateway to Monument Square at the center of the City. The 160,000 square foot building accommodates the Mason Gross School of the Arts, the Bloustein School of Planning and Public Policy, and the Center for Urban Policy Research. Underground parking for 400 cars is provided.

The art school program comprises painting and drawing studios, galleries, offices, and classrooms, as well as printmaking and photography labs, and video recording spaces. The planning schools include offices and classrooms, computer labs and a 160-seat auditorium.

The different components of the program are contrasted in the elevations and massing of the building. Significantly, the art school wing of the structure is four stories in height, while the planning schools are housed in a five-story wing. The difference in scale is a specific response to the needs of the programs; the space required for the completion and display of large-scale work, as well as for the ventilation of the studios and labs, required greater ceiling heights in the art school wing. The schools are, however, unified on the ground floor, sharing a central lobby, atrium, auditorium, and staircase, which functions as the primary circulation spine for the building.

The building is designed to reinforce the rhythm of buildings along Livingston Avenue, and to define a series of frames for viewing the urban context. To this end, major components of the art school and planning school project beyond the main building block to meet the sidewalk. The space between the blocks is an academic courtyard that provides the main entry to the building and functions as a "stage" open to the street. A sculpture by Alice Aycock, an elevated table, activates this space.

Materials utilized include a warm red brick with dark and light panelization, and exposed steel and aluminum structures. The urban wall of the red brick is pierced by the various grid structures of steel and glass.

New Brunswick, NJ, 1995

Civic Square I: Center for the Arts and Planning at Rutgers University

Front elevation.

Rear elevation.

Opposite, entry and court.

Student lounge.

Main lobby.

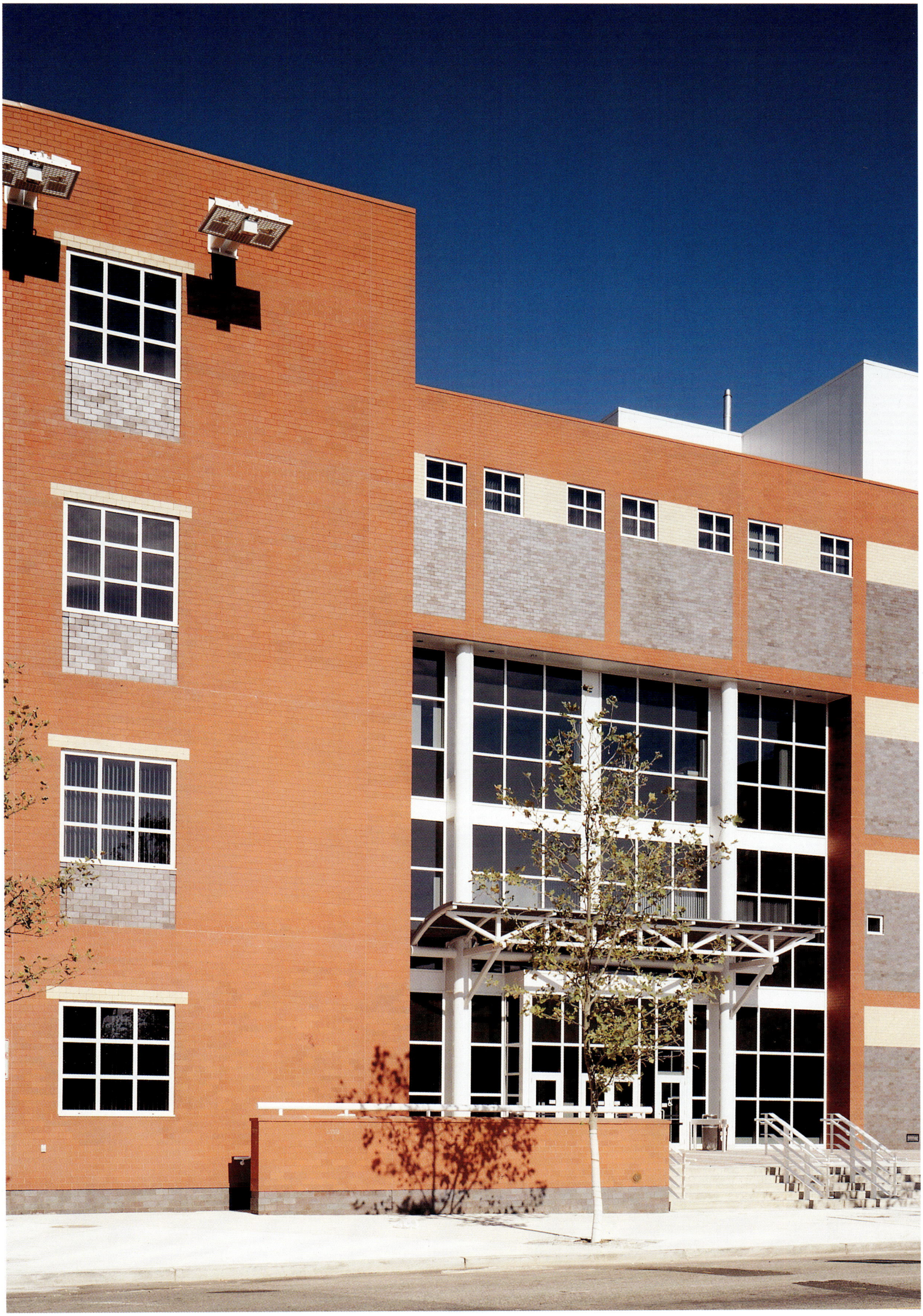

First floor plan.

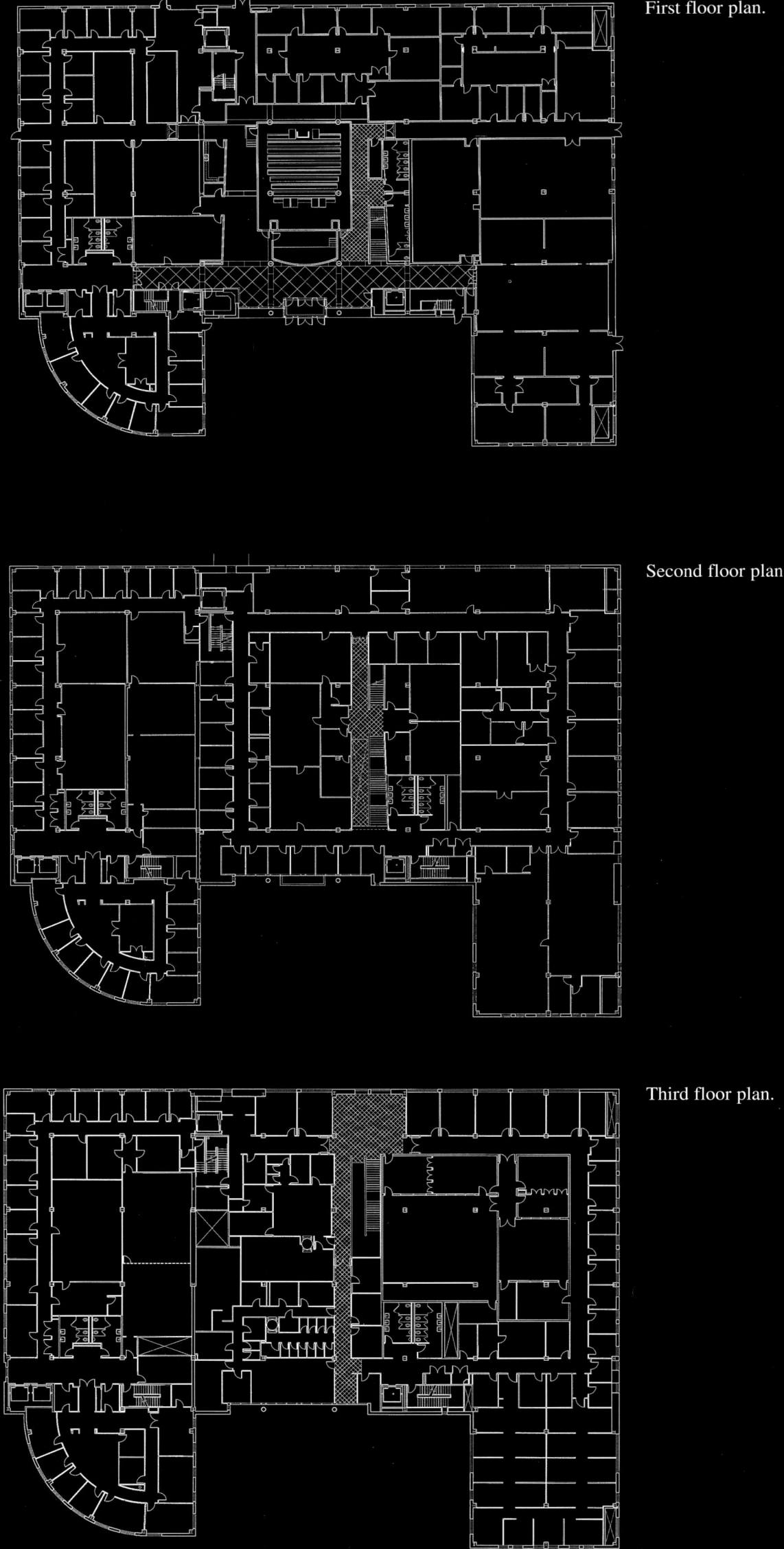

Second floor plan.

Third floor plan.

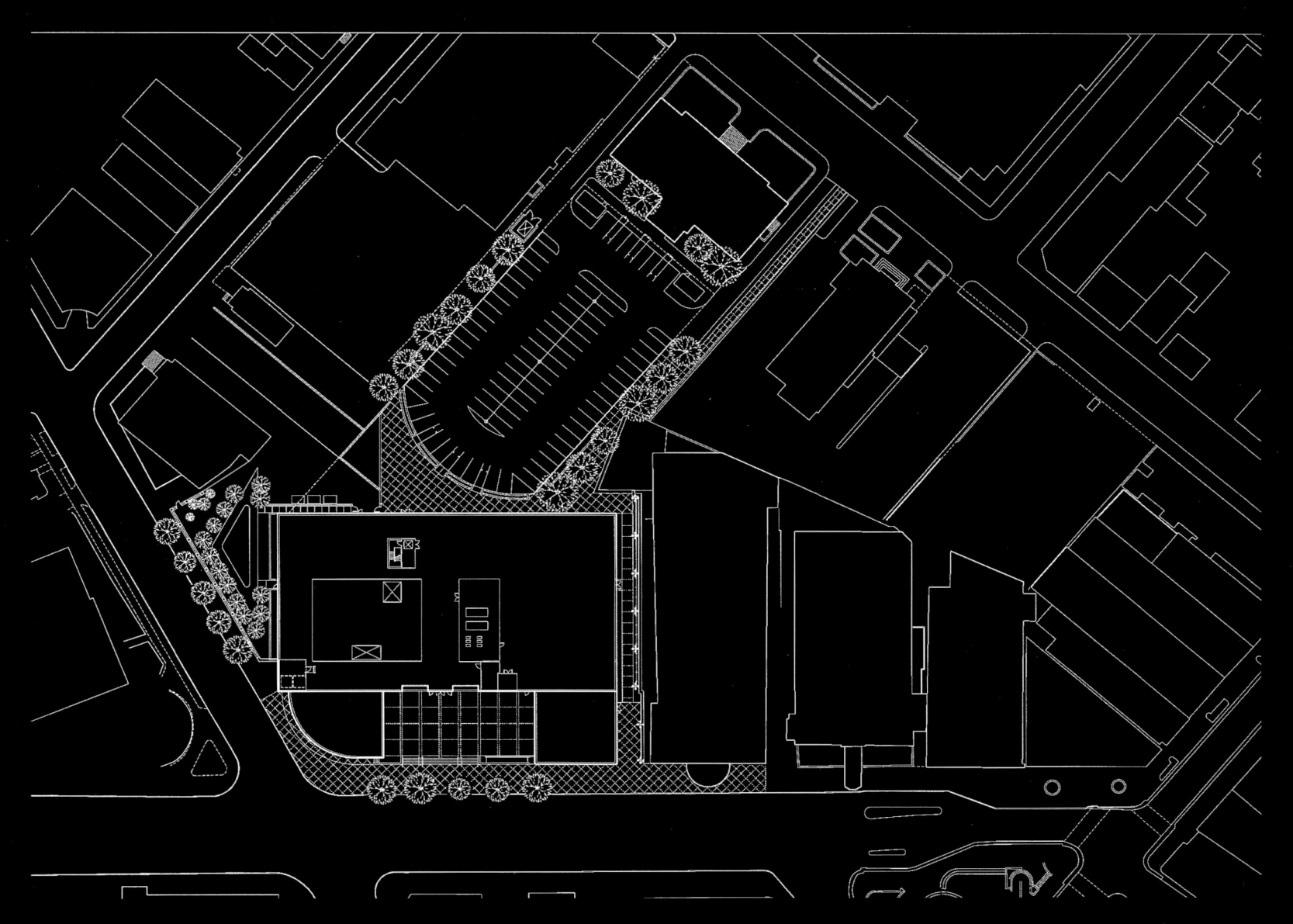

Site plan.

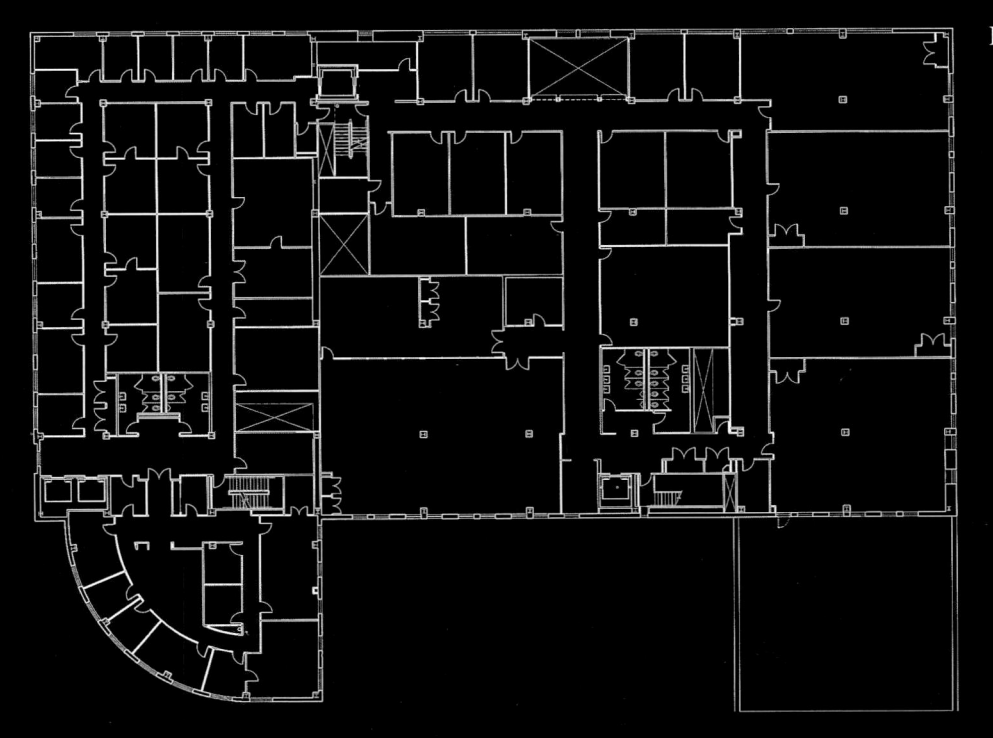

Fourth floor plan.

Partial axonometric.

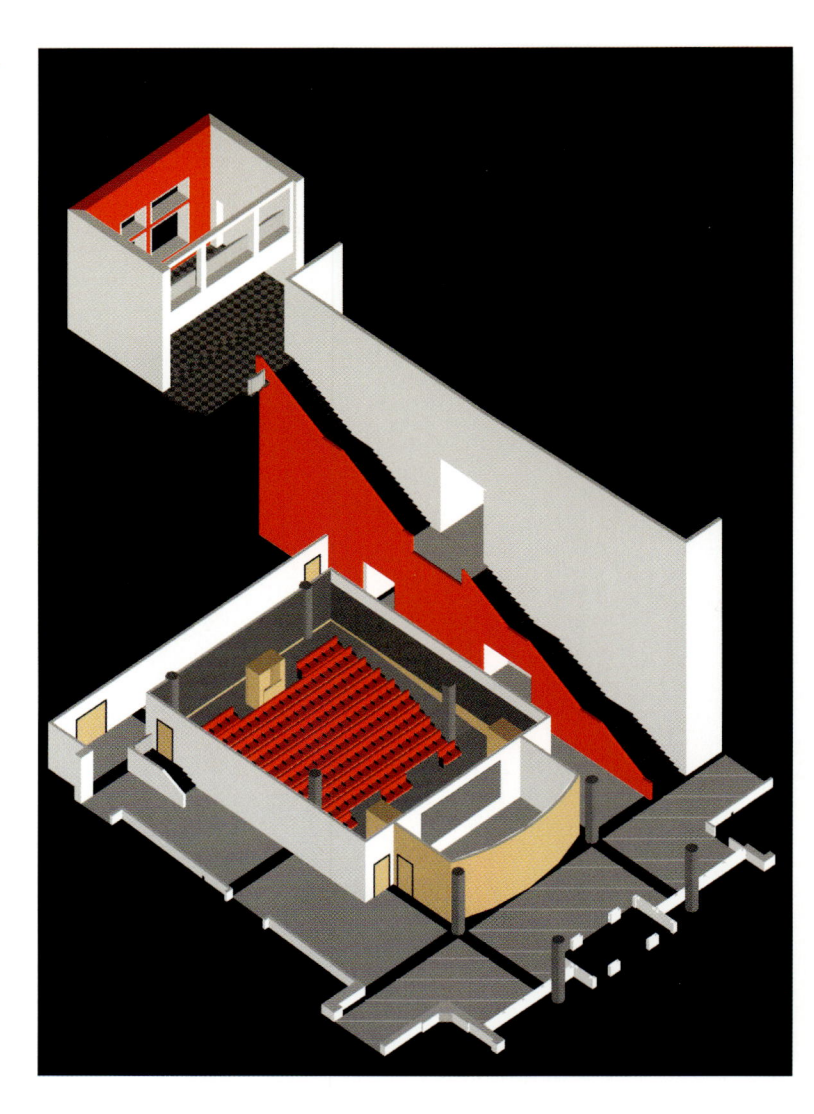

View of stair.

Main auditorium.

The New Jersey Historical Society is responsible for collecting, preserving and interpreting the rich political, social, cultural and economic history of the State of New Jersey. Through its collections, exhibitions, library, publications, and programming, the Society strives to serve as a major cultural voice. The relocation from its former building to a new site in the center of Newark, the Essex Club, facilitates this mission.

As the first step in the process of relocating a major cultural institution, the Board of Governors commissioned the architects to prepare a feasibility study and preservation plan for the Essex Club in 1993. Based on this plan, the architects developed a design to renovate and restore the circa 1926 Georgian Revival clubhouse to serve as headquarters for the institution, which operates a historical museum, library, and archives. Major grants were utilized to accomplish the recommended work. One of those grants carried specific requirements for providing barrier-free access and appropriate environmental control systems. The project was carefully reviewed by the granting agencies and other state and local agencies with jurisdiction, including the State Historic Preservation Office and local code officials.

In the renovation of this former businessmen's club, major interior spaces were adapted to meet the needs of the Historical Society while the fine historical architectural details were preserved and restored. The main dining room was converted to an exhibit space for rotating exhibits; the tap room was turned into a meeting room; a library and reading room with expansive views of the downtown was created in the space that formerly housed a corporate suite; the squash courts and their spectators' gallery became archival storage; and the walnut-paneled lounge now houses exhibits from the Historical Society's permanent collection. The project also included exterior restoration of the five-story, Neoclassical building; the addition of new museum-quality environmental control systems; and extensive improvements to make the facility code-compliant.

Opposite, former Essex Club
Park Place elevation.

Newark, NJ, 1997

New Jersey Historical Society

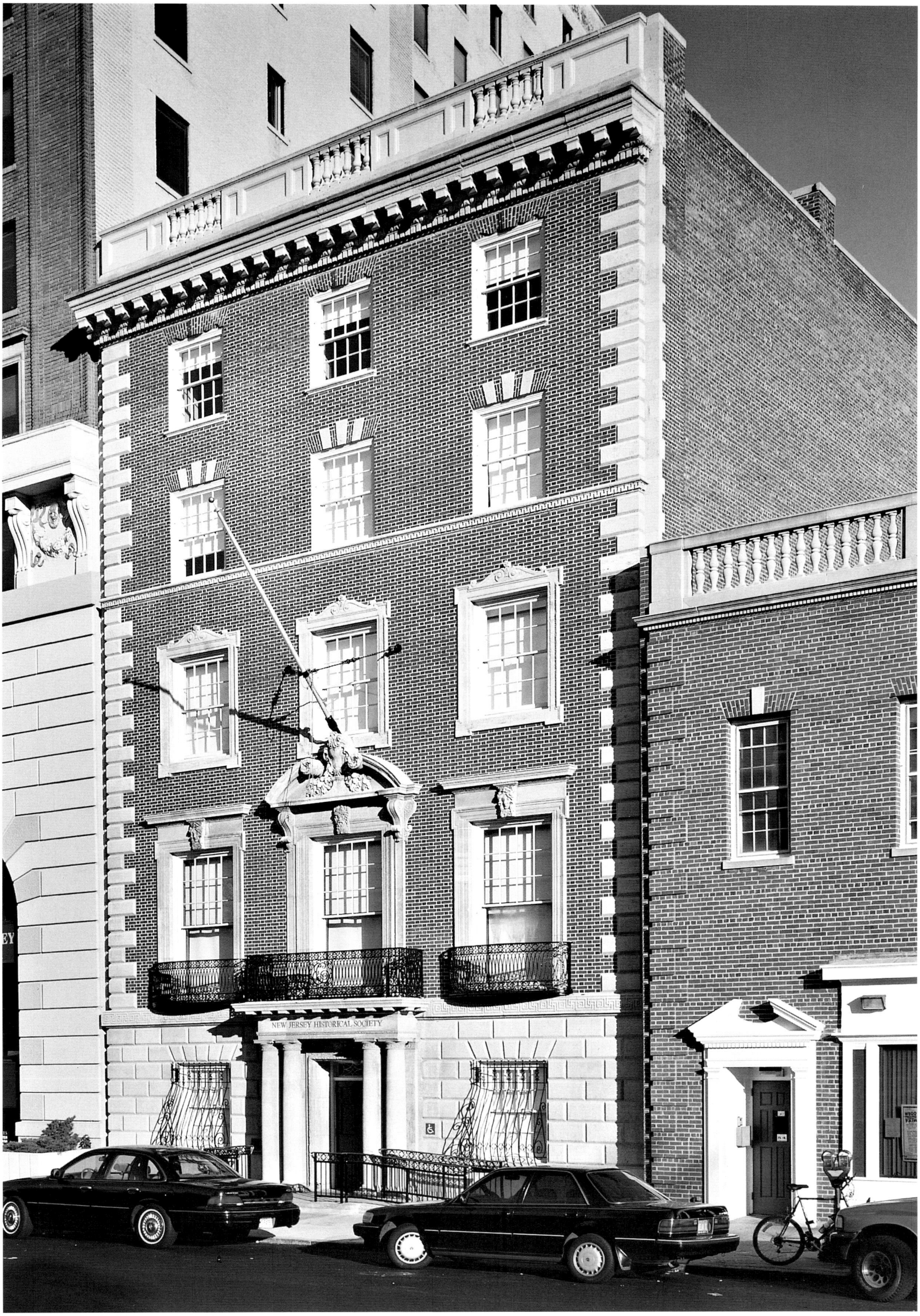
NEW JERSEY HISTORICAL SOCIETY

Monumental stair,
second floor.

Permanent exhibition area.

Library and Reading Room,
fifth floor.

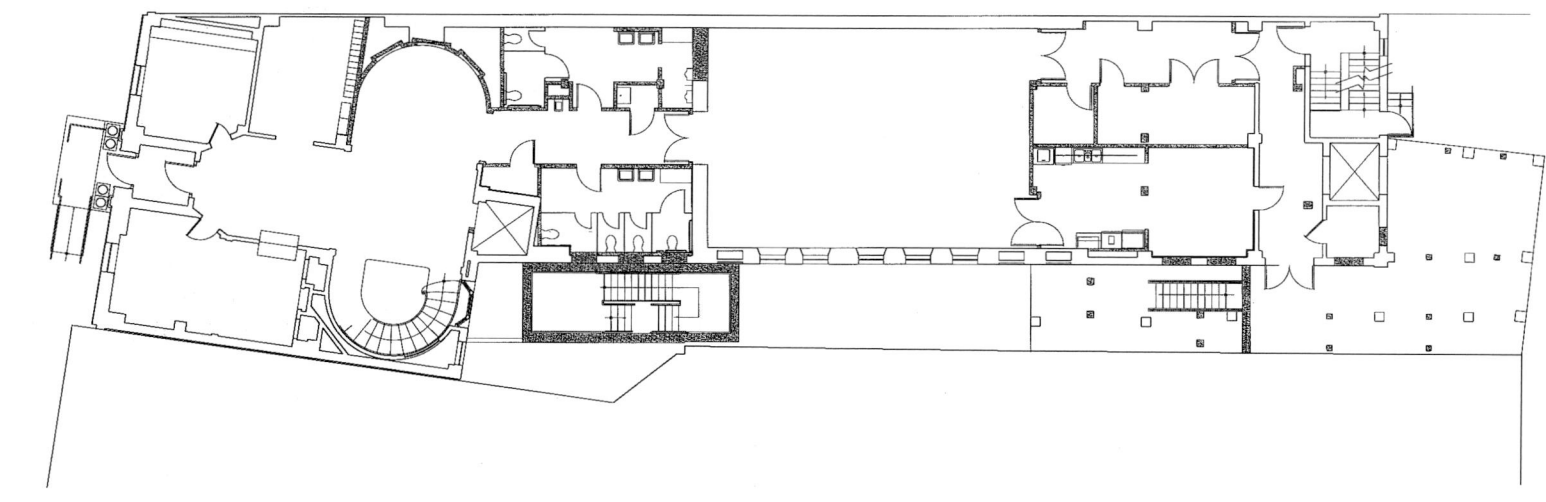

First floor plan.

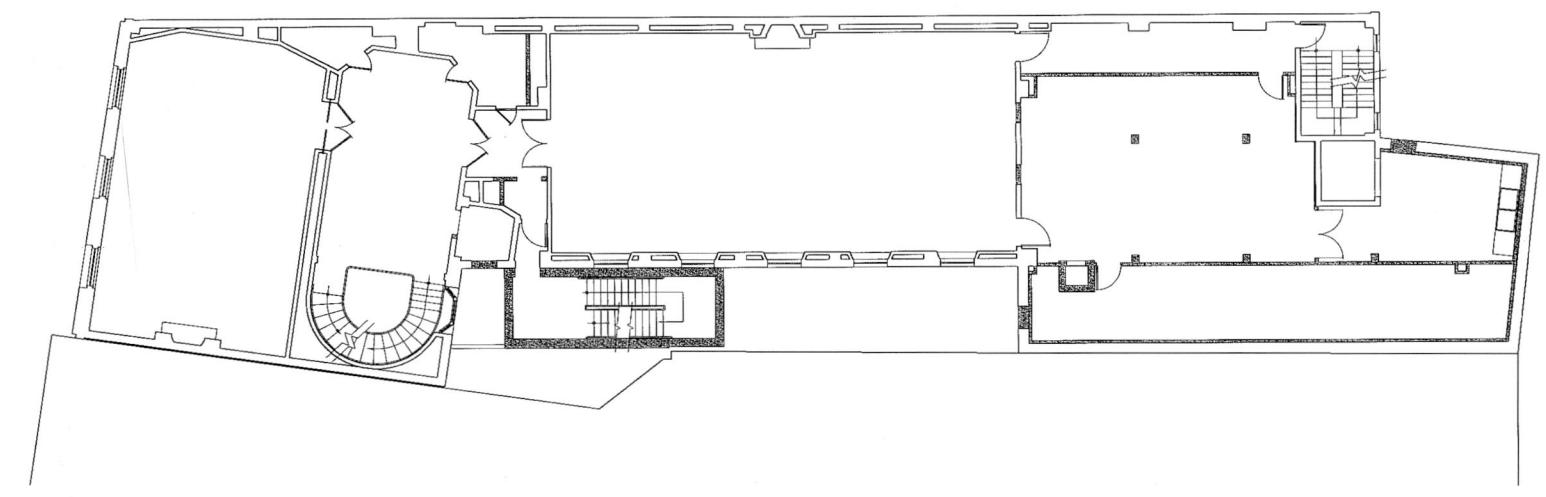

Second floor plan.

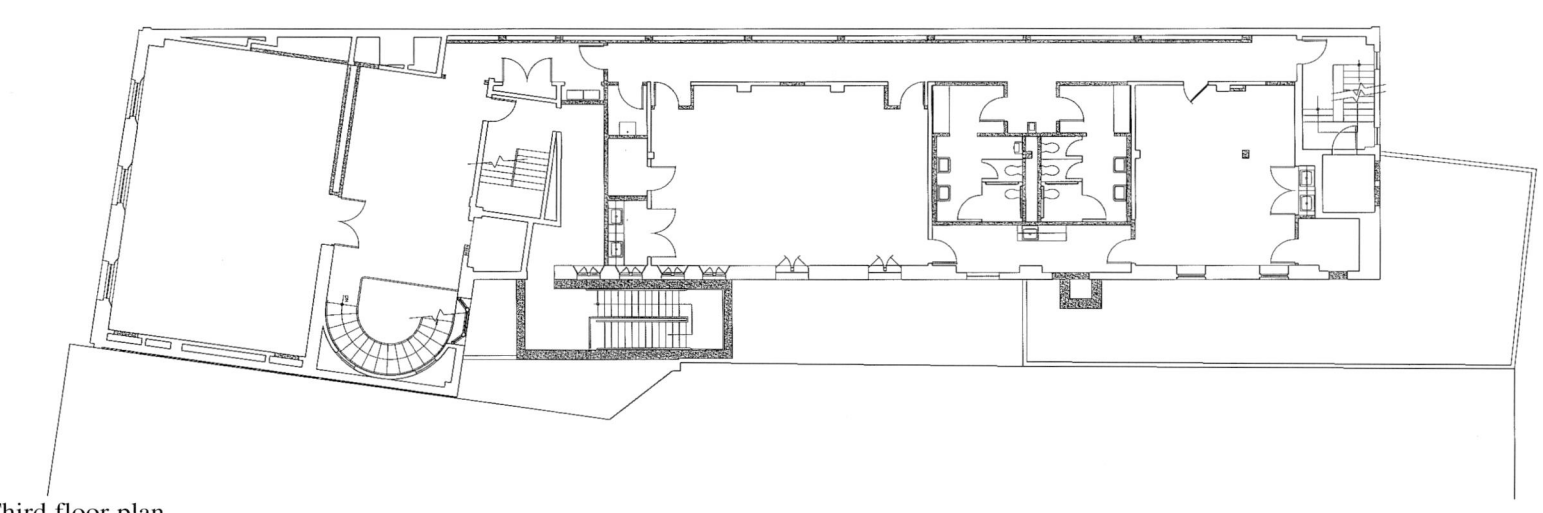

Third floor plan.

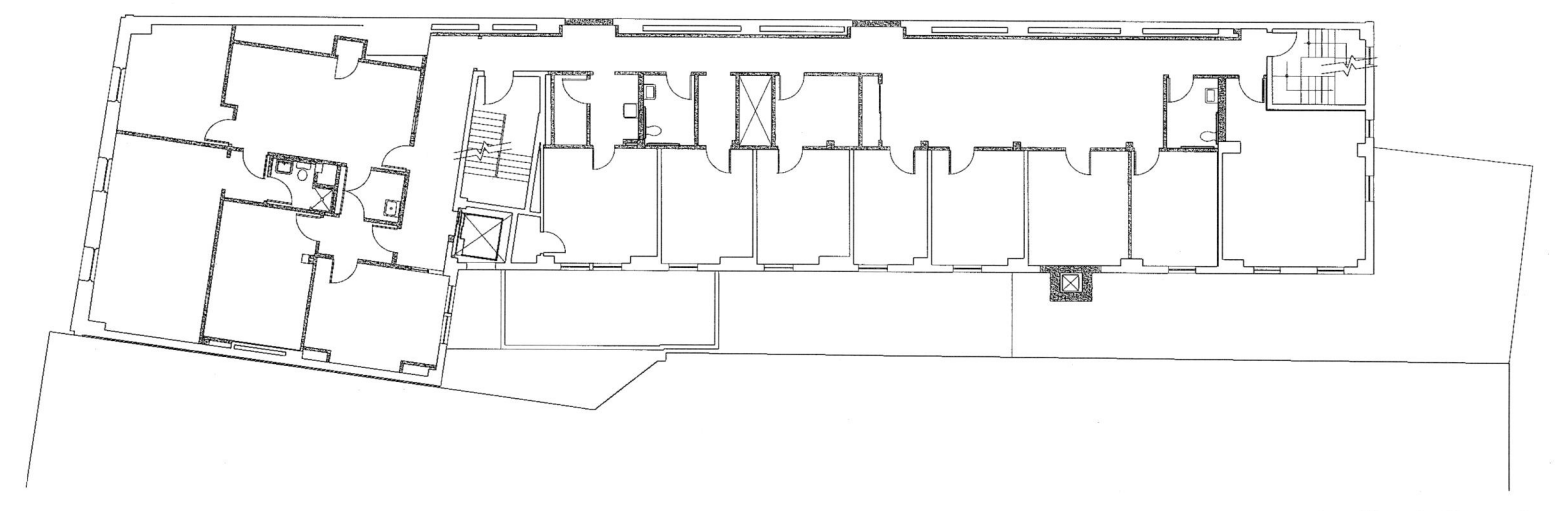

Fourth floor plan.

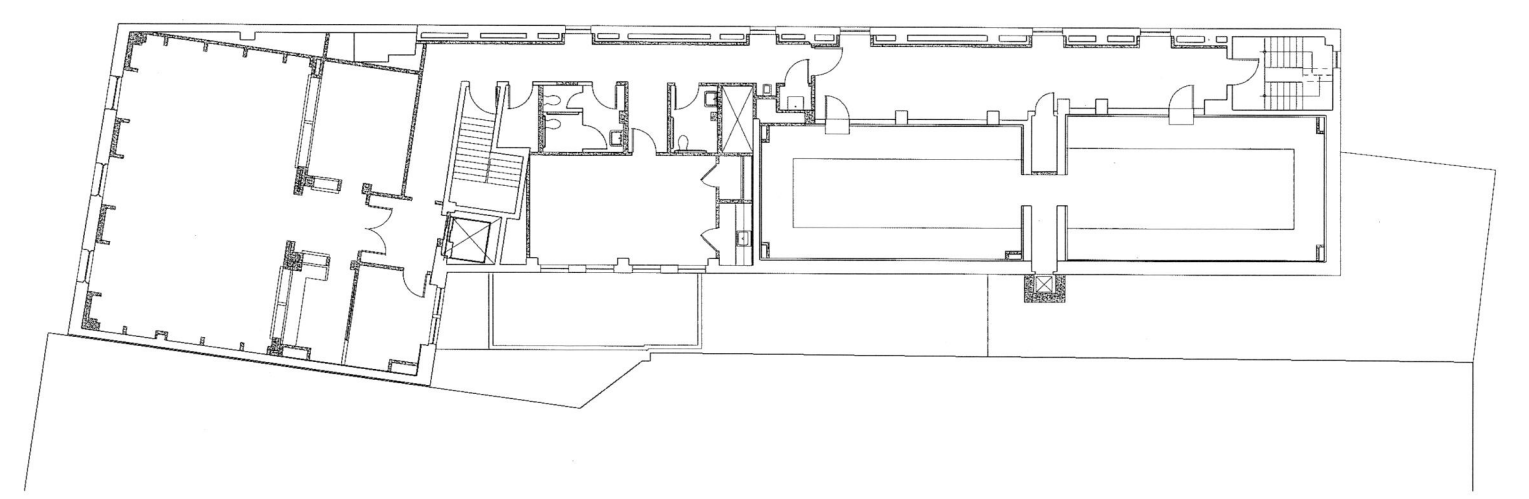

Fifth floor plan.

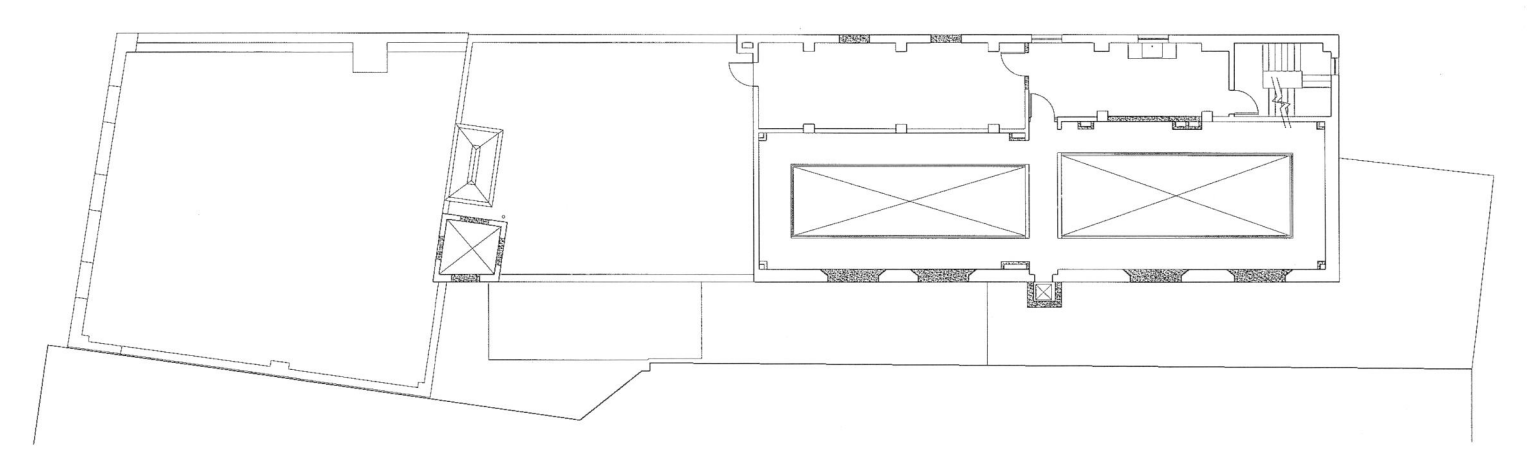

Sixth floor plan.

Archivial storage,
fifth and sixth floors.

Main exhibit space,
second floor.

Meeting room,
first floor.

The F.M. Kirby Shakespeare Theatre, located at Drew University's Bowne Hall, is set in a grove of trees bordering an oval "bowl" at the center of the campus. Bowne Hall was originally built as a gymnasium in 1908, and has been the home of the Shakespeare Festival, one of New Jersey's premiere theatre companies, for many years. The renovated building was designed to accommodate the New Jersey Shakespeare Festival's productions of classic plays, with additional use by the Drew University Drama Department during the academic year, as well as music and dance events. However, it was important to the University that significant elements of the original building be retained in the new theatre design to preserve the overall campus plan.

The solution was to accommodate the university requirements that the historic building exterior be preserved and to establish a dialogue between old and new that reflected the nature of this theatre's work. The "L" shaped addition brackets the original building, allowing the new and existing to have discernable identities. The addition on two sides houses the increased seating needs as well as new lobby, office, and board meeting room spaces. The exterior of the addition is finished with a Roman brick veneer that matches the original brick of Bowne Hall. In addition, the building is reoriented to the east with a new entry and fore court. This court, used for intermissions and receptions, connects to a campus portal to the south and the bowl on the east. In the evening, the lobby and bay window act as a sort of lantern, illuminating the campus with the theatre's dynamic social program.

The reconfigured building includes a 308-seat theatre with a thrust stage, box office and lobby, rehearsal room, dressing rooms, support offices, and a board meeting room. The interior of the house, restructured within the existing three exterior walls, creates an intimate, focused space, which maintains audience engagement with actors. Excellent sightlines, barrier free access, and sound isolation were vital requirements for the new theatre, as well as a trapped stage with lift. Theatre equipment, including light instrument booms, catwalks, and speaker clusters, along with exposed structure, are juxtaposed with the smooth plaster walls and ceiling planes of the house.

Madison, NJ, 1998

F.M. Kirby Shakespeare Theatre at Drew University

Front elevation.

Lobby.

New entrance.

View of lobby.

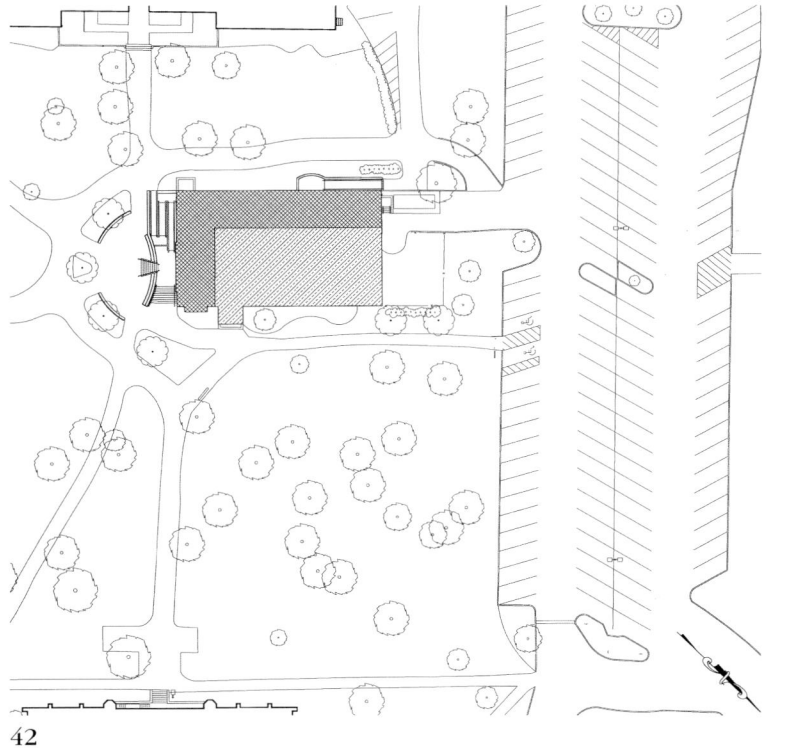

Site plan.

View of the house and stage.

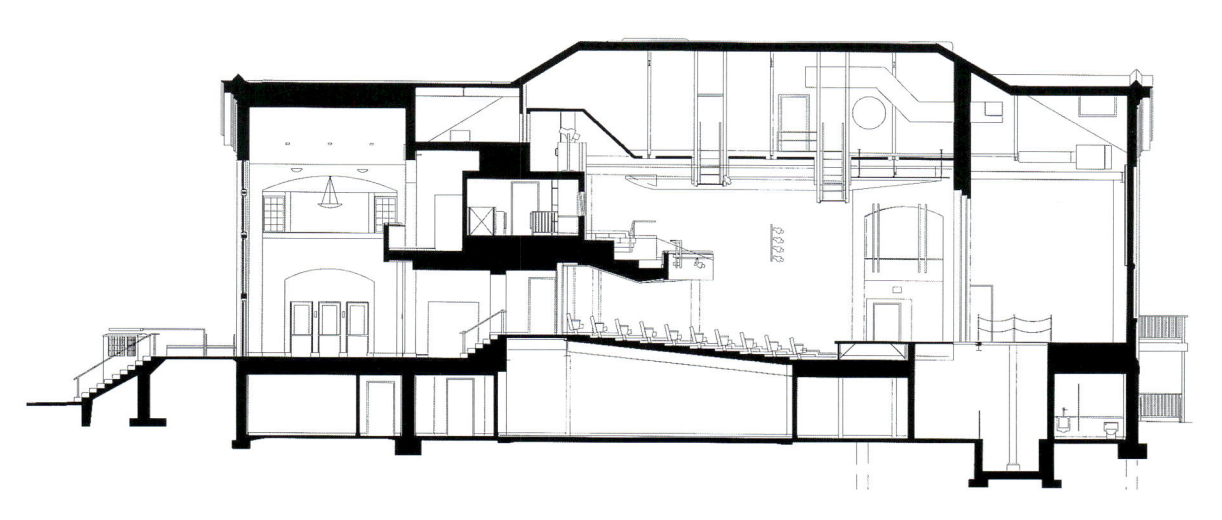

Longitudinal section.

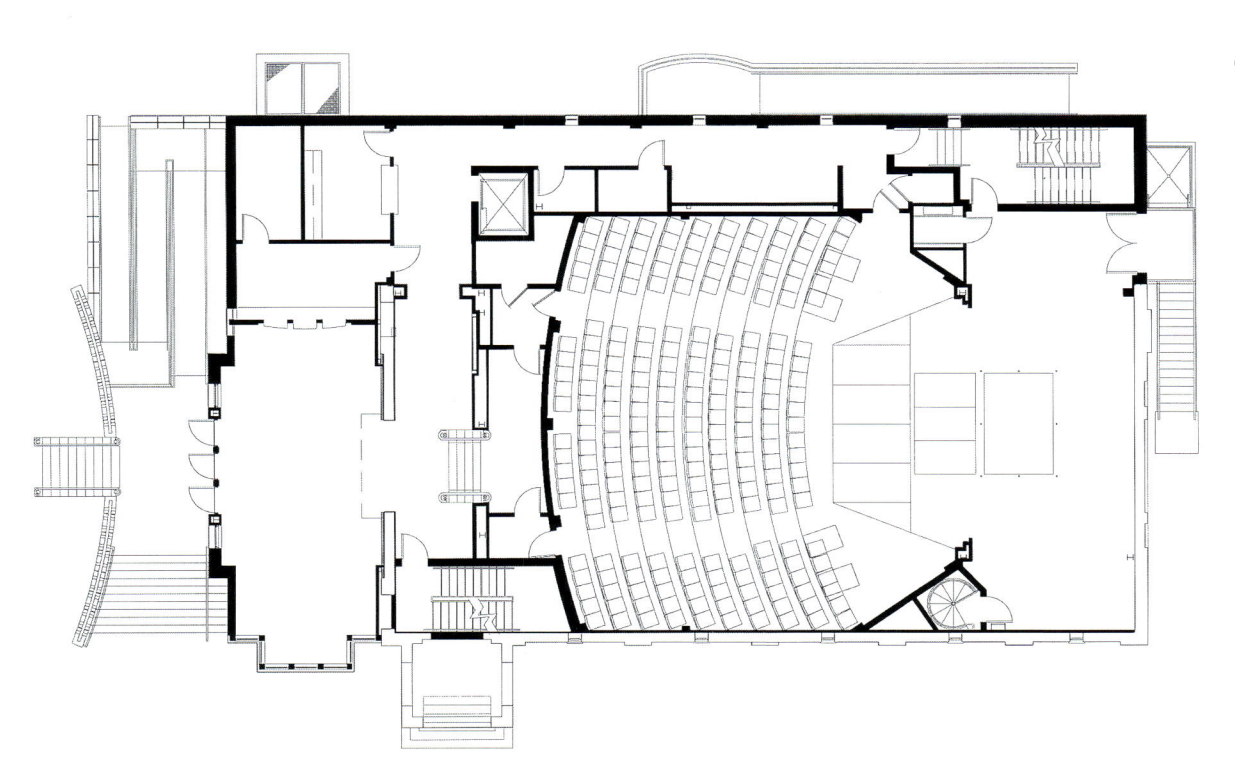

Ground floor plan.

43

Stone Works

The New Jersey State House, begun in 1792, is the second-oldest State House in the United States in continuous use. The original building, a two-story masonry structure on a bluff overlooking the Delaware River, housed all three branches of government. There were two legislative chambers on the first floor, while the Governor and the Judiciary shared the second floor. This building partially survives and now houses the Governor's office.

The firm's association with the New Jersey State House project began in 1981 with the preparation of a Legislative Space Study, followed in 1984 by an Executive Space Study for the other half of the building. In 1984, the Executive and Legislative branches engaged the architects to undertake a Master Plan. The Master Plan was implemented over a period of seventeen years. The project has been realized in several major phases, beginning with the design of temporary quarters for the Legislature in the State House Annex.

This project presented the firm with a unique opportunity to study and reinterpret for the public a collection of spectacular historic spaces, representing a variety of architectural periods, each with its own unique identity. The General Assembly Chamber is representative of Late Victorian exuberance. Work in this room included restoration of the decorative plaster, stained glass, gold leaf and oak millwork. The highlight of the room is the restored brass light fixtures, including the massive chandelier. The Senate Chamber is more academic in its design. Certain elements such as the decorative plaster, gold leaf, stained glass, and millwork posed restoration challenges similar to the Assembly Chamber. Other elements, including the oil on canvas murals and the *scagliola* (faux marble) wainscot and columns, were unique to the Senate Chamber.

Among the treasures uncovered were fragments of a painted ceiling from an earlier era that were preserved in a meeting room adjacent to the Assembly Chamber, and a remarkable barrel vaulted ceiling in the former Supreme Court Chamber that now houses the Senate Majority Conference Room. New offices for the Legislative leadership were inserted into restored rooms near the Chambers, while unused basement space was captured to create meeting and work space for other part-time Legislators, off the Chambers' floor and out of the public eye.

The new South Addition, a 30,000 square foot Legislative staff building, provides a new entry from the parking to the south. The granite-clad structure is a solid base that supports the Neoclassical buildings above it, while providing new views and access through a series of carved-out interior volumes.

Trenton, NJ, 1991

Legislative Chambers and Addition to the New Jersey State House

View from the south showing addition and restored legislative chambers.

New lobby.

Senate stair.

View from new lobby to south facade.

Opposite, Senate Chamber.

48

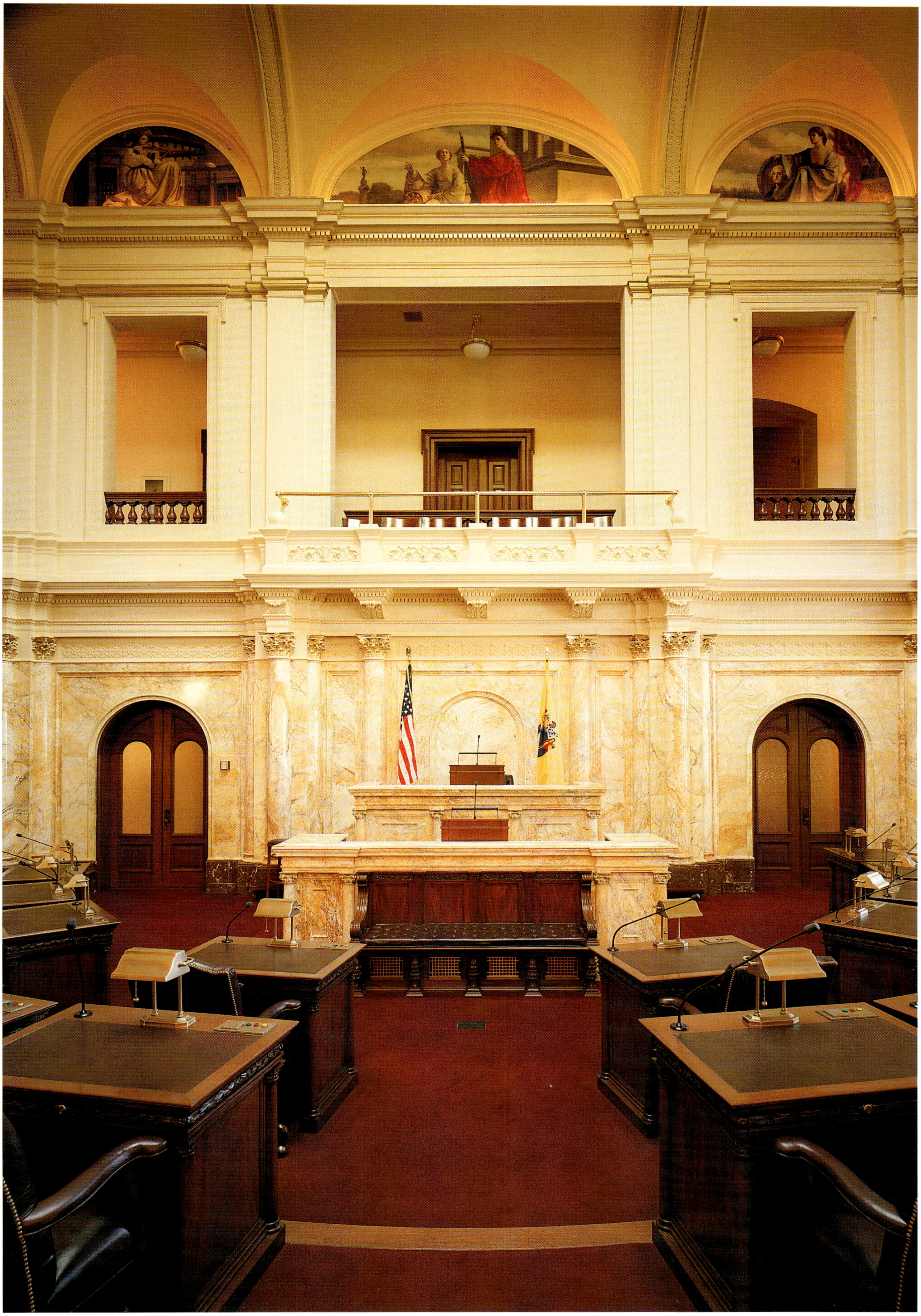

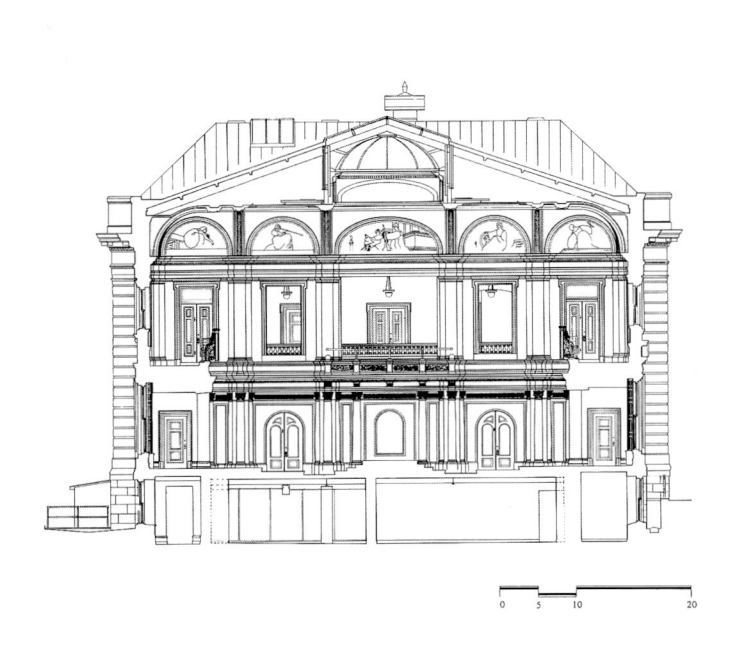

South elevation, Senate.

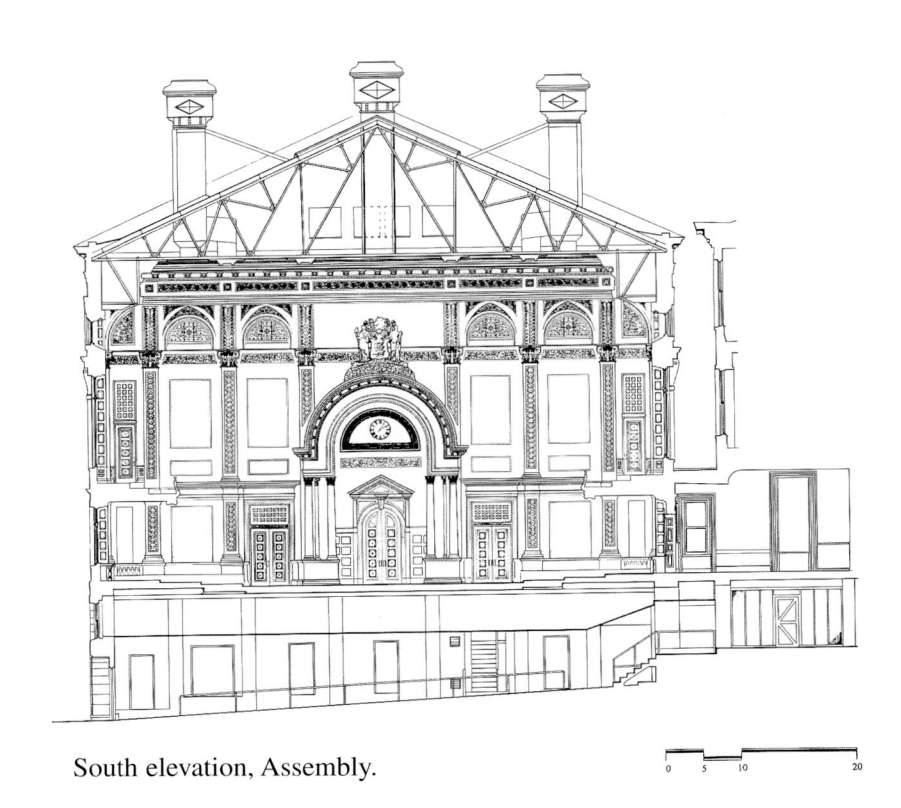

South elevation, Assembly.

Section through Senate wing.

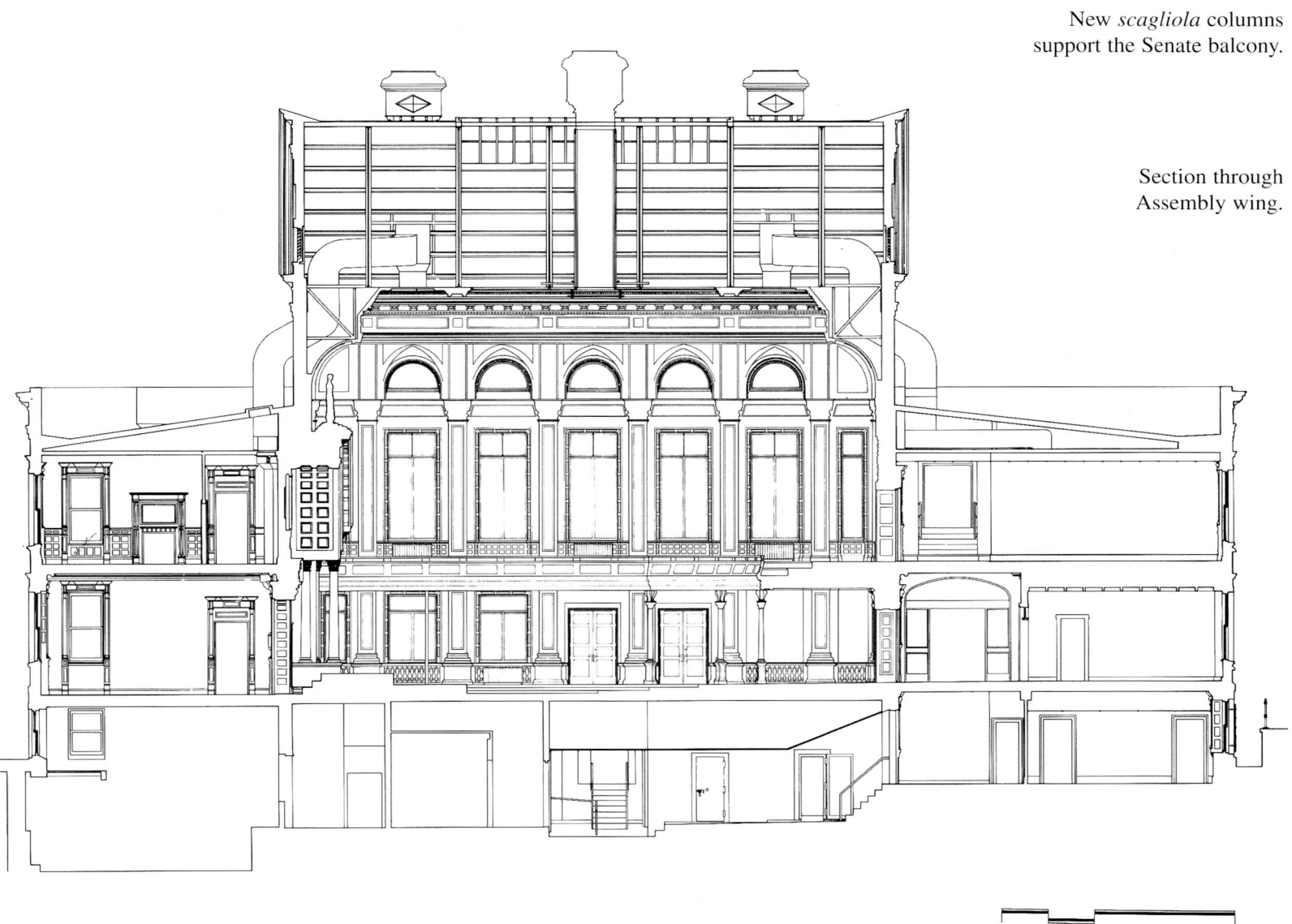

New *scagliola* columns support the Senate balcony.

Section through Assembly wing.

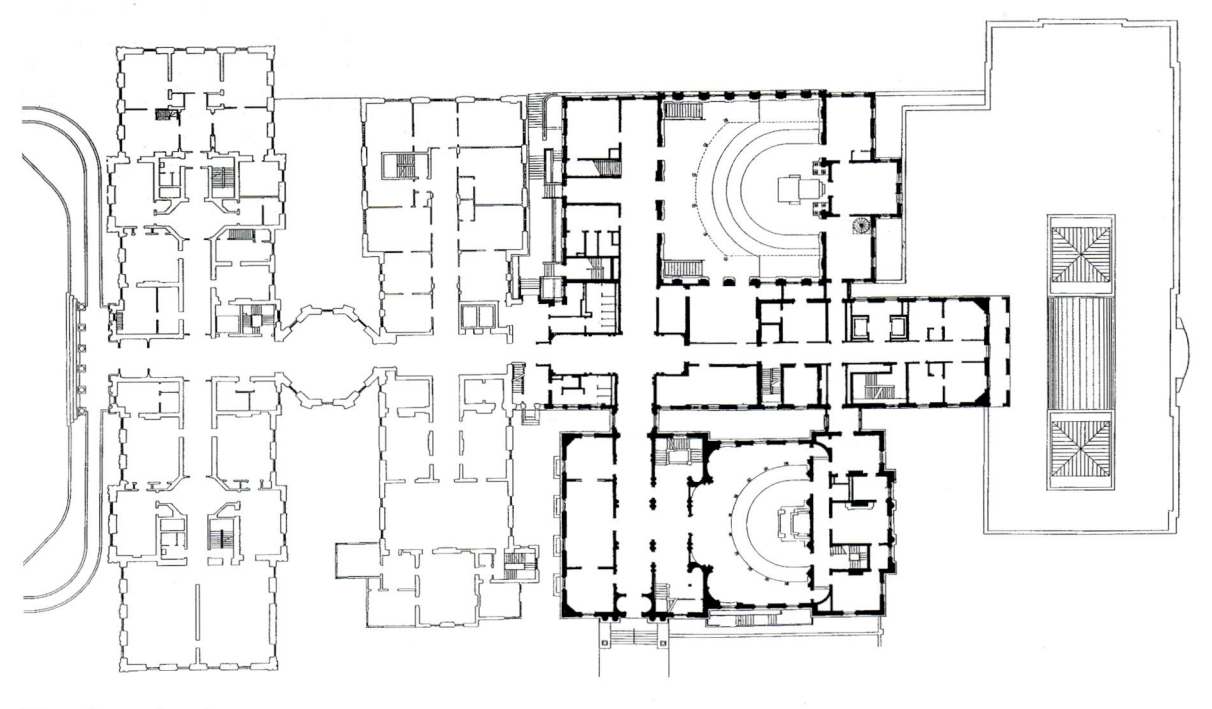

First floor showing
legislative areas.

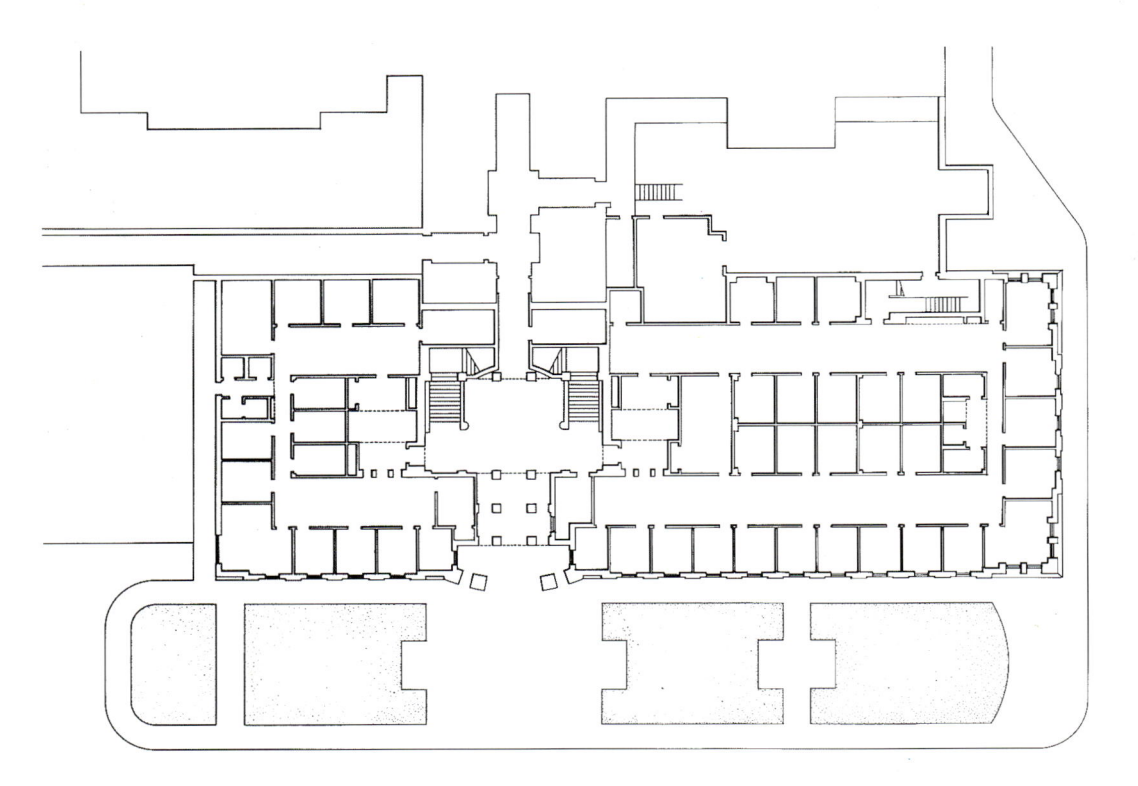

South addition,
ground floor plan.

State House Annex

State House

South elevation.

Assembly Chamber.

New Assembly Committee Room.

This addition to a 1930s Shingle Style house is located on the waterfront of the north shore of Fisher's Island. The site has views to the west between a pair of low hillocks to North Dumpling Lighthouse, and north over Long Island Sound toward the Connecticut coast.

The goal of this project was to make a place that is dynamically interwoven into its island environment. Through the placement of granite walls that extend and abstract the foundation of the existing house, a labyrinthine series of rooms and passages are carved in the landscape. The main pool, a 20- by 44-foot rectangle, has a finely detailed disappearing edge on its ocean side, with a trough and scupper that feed a smaller semicircular pool below. The floor of the pool has a cosmological map executed in marble mosaic inlaid in natural plaster. To further highlight the nature of the site, the stairways and diving board are located to give direct views of the lighthouse on the sound and of spires on the Connecticut coast.

The spaces, of differing levels of light, closure, and view, are intersected by structures of aluminum, steel, fabric, and teak that relate to the ships and airplanes passing by the site. The physical sensations of descent, gravity, enclosure, and immersion created by the granite and water are contrasted with the sensation of flight suggested by the tensile canopy of stainless steel and awning fabric that shades the poolside. These physical sensations simultaneously express the conflicting desires of human nature, to be grounded and to be free.

Fisher's Island, NY, 1993

Pool, Pool House and Landscape II

View of 1930s house with new pool and pool house.

View of the wing.

View of granite walls
with wing.

56

View toward the lighthouse.

Plan.
1. Changing Room
2. Shower
3. Equipment

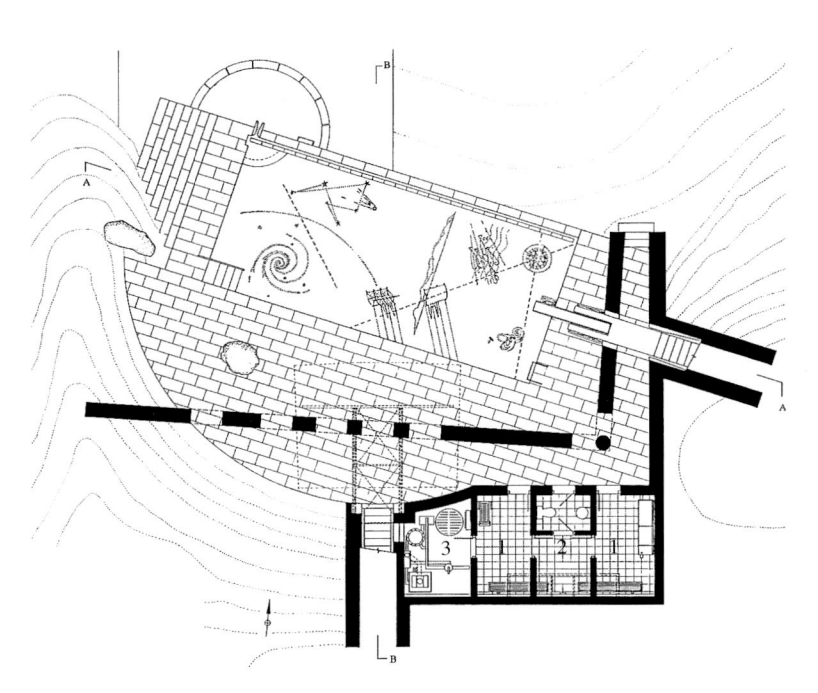

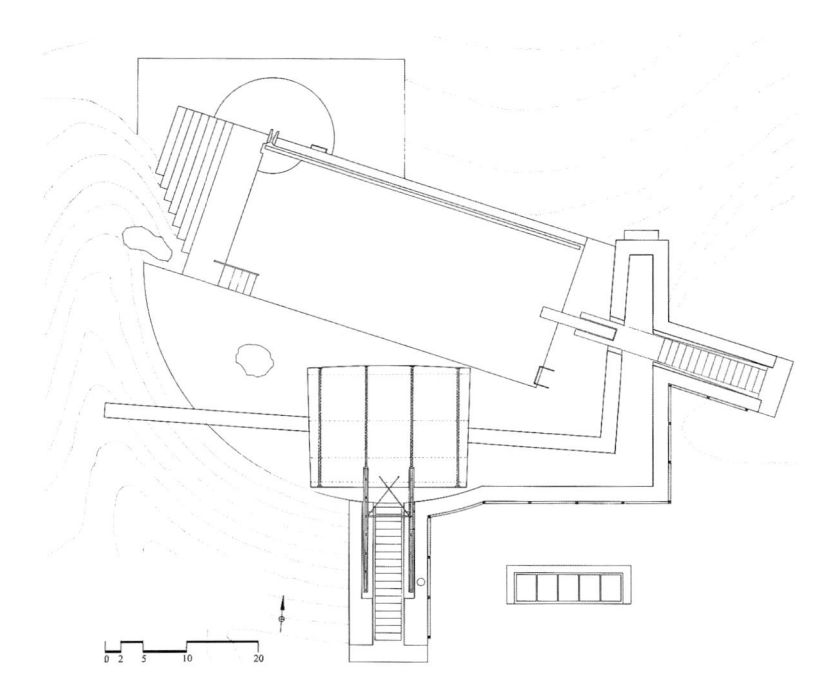

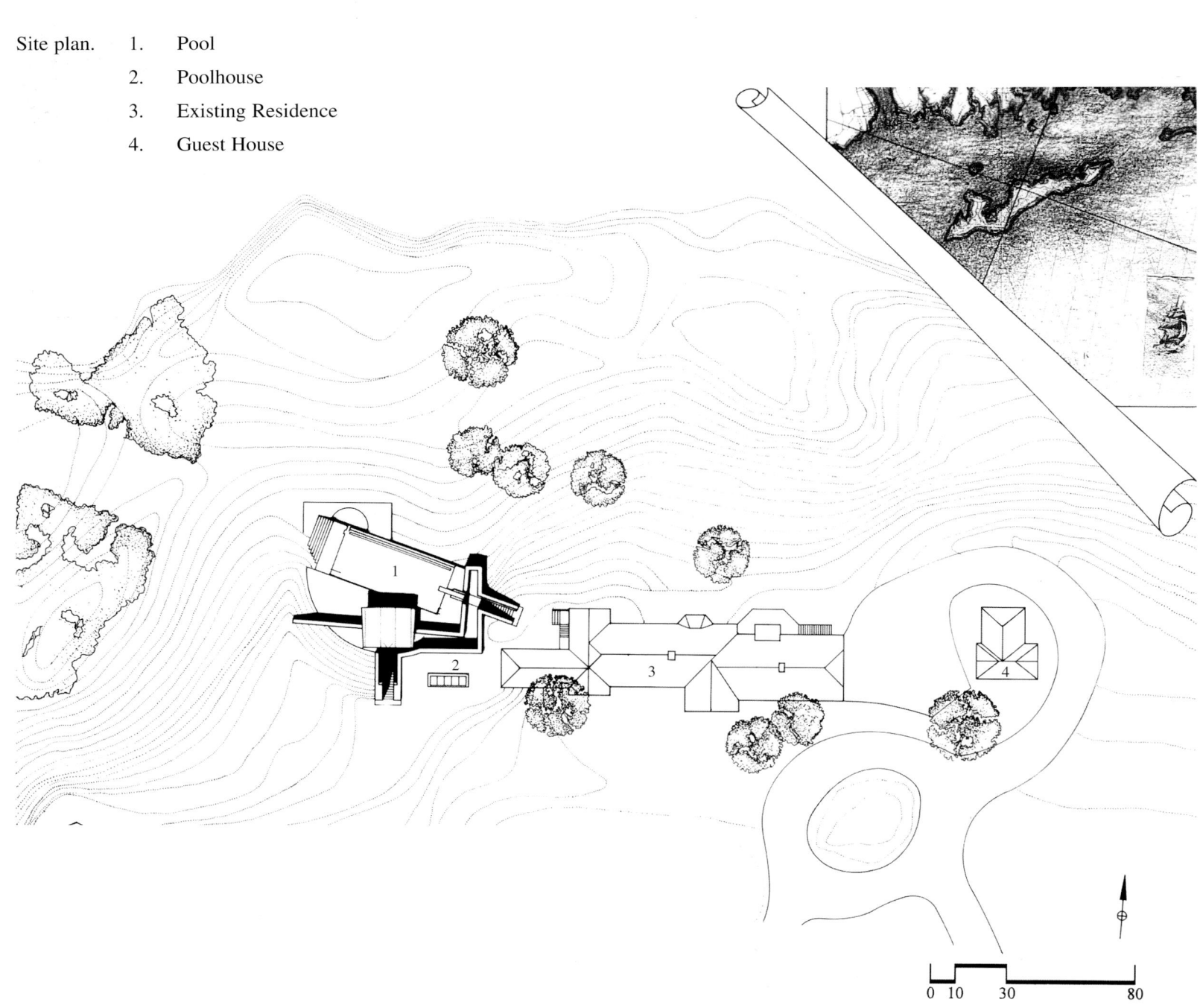

Roof plan.

Site plan.
1. Pool
2. Poolhouse
3. Existing Residence
4. Guest House

View of wing and pool floor.

View to the north.

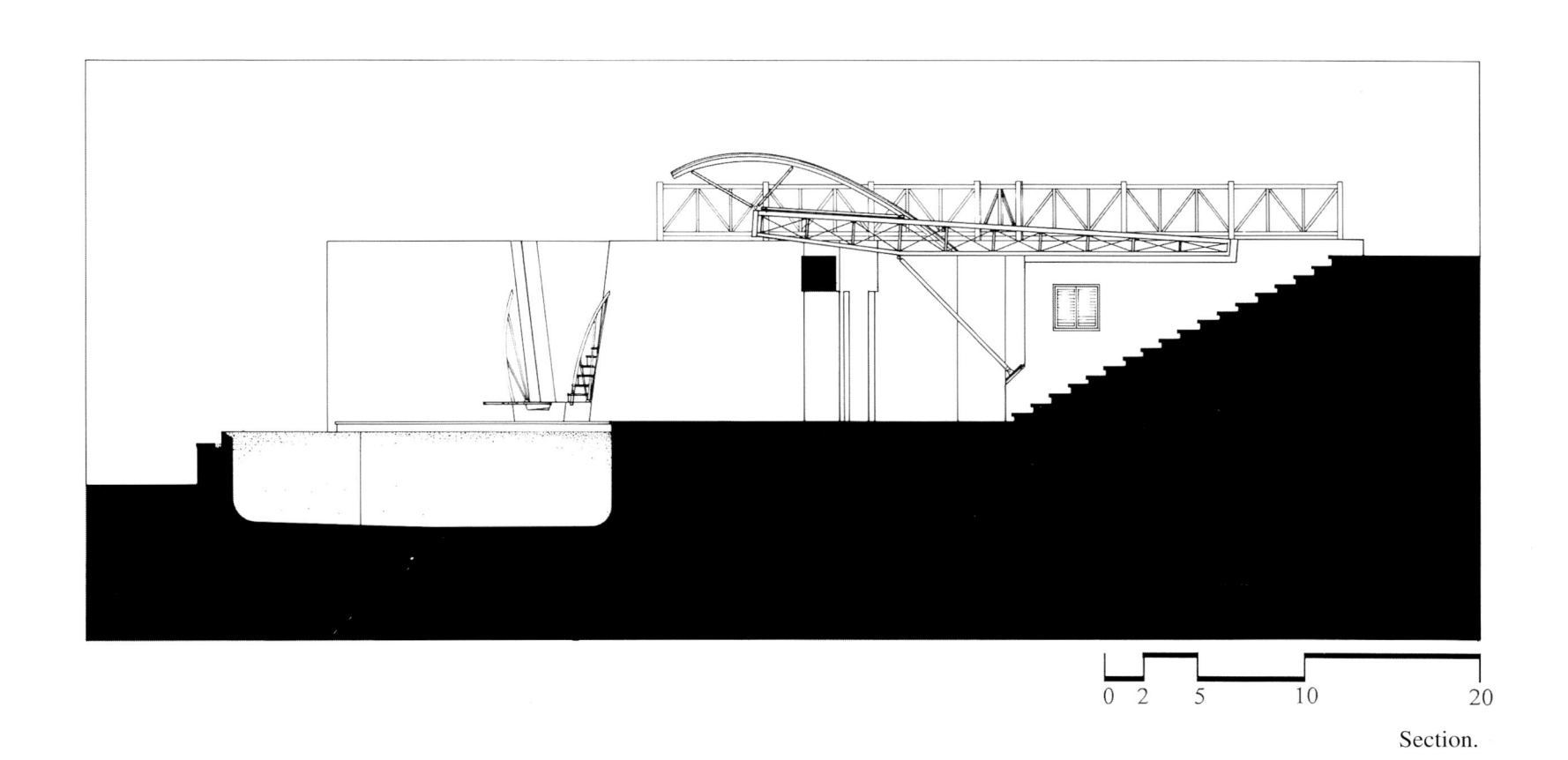

Section.

59

Designed by Ralph Adams Cram and begun in 1911, Princeton University's Graduate College is perhaps the foremost example of collegiate gothic architecture in the United States. Set in a wooded landscape designed by Beatrix Jones Farrand and bordered by the Springdale Golf Club, the Graduate College is a single building of nearly 150,000 square feet, but composed of a number of elements including Cleveland Tower; Wyman House (the Dean's residence); dormitory wings; and major public spaces (Procter Hall, the Common Room, and Van Dyke Library).

The firm began work at the Graduate College in 1986 when a comprehensive historical and existing conditions survey was commissioned by the University. It was concluded that the building materials were of exceptional quality, however, due to 78 years of heavy usage, they were in need of renewal. The infrastructure was at the end of its useful life, and, most importantly, the building did not meet New Jersey's life safety standards.

Recognizing the architectural importance of the complex, the University directed the design team to preserve the original plan and architectural features, while upgrading the various systems. The work included complete heating, plumbing, and electrical system replacement, installation of a new sprinkler system; installation of computer wiring and data connections in every bedroom and study; and repair and restoration of all finishes in the dormitory suites including woodwork, plaster, stone, and metals.

The work brought with it many challenges, interesting solutions, and considerable reward. The aim of the project was to make the installation of new systems as inconspicuous as possible, and to allow the architectural beauty of the virtually unchanged complex to take center stage. In order to achieve this goal, piping was routed through the few original chases, student closets, and existing dropped ceilings above bathrooms and stair landings. Where new risers were absolutely necessary, corner pilasters were added with new woodwork returning around them to match the original. Utility distribution occurred in the space beneath the wood floors to keep the cutting of asbestos containing plaster to a minimum.

Six years after the rehabilitation of the Graduate College was completed, the firm returned to the Graduate College to restore Cleveland Tower, the centerpiece of Ralph Adams Cram's medieval masterpiece. Over two hundred carved pieces of decorative limestone were replaced in the restoration. The stone repair, cleaning, and repointing will ensure that the tower will continue to serve as a campus and community landmark for the next one hundred years.

The necessity of renovating older campus building often results in a "maintenance mindset" centered only on the pipes and wires, while ignoring the special potential of individual buildings. In this case, Princeton University viewed the Graduate College as a building of national significance worthy of careful preservation. The project resulted in a building that looks much as it did when it first opened, ready to receive future generations of students. It also improved the quality of both academic and residential life at the Graduate College, and now serves as a model to other colleges undertaking similar work with their historic campuses.

Opposite, Cleveland Tower pinnacle.

Princeton, NJ, 1993

Princeton University Graduate College

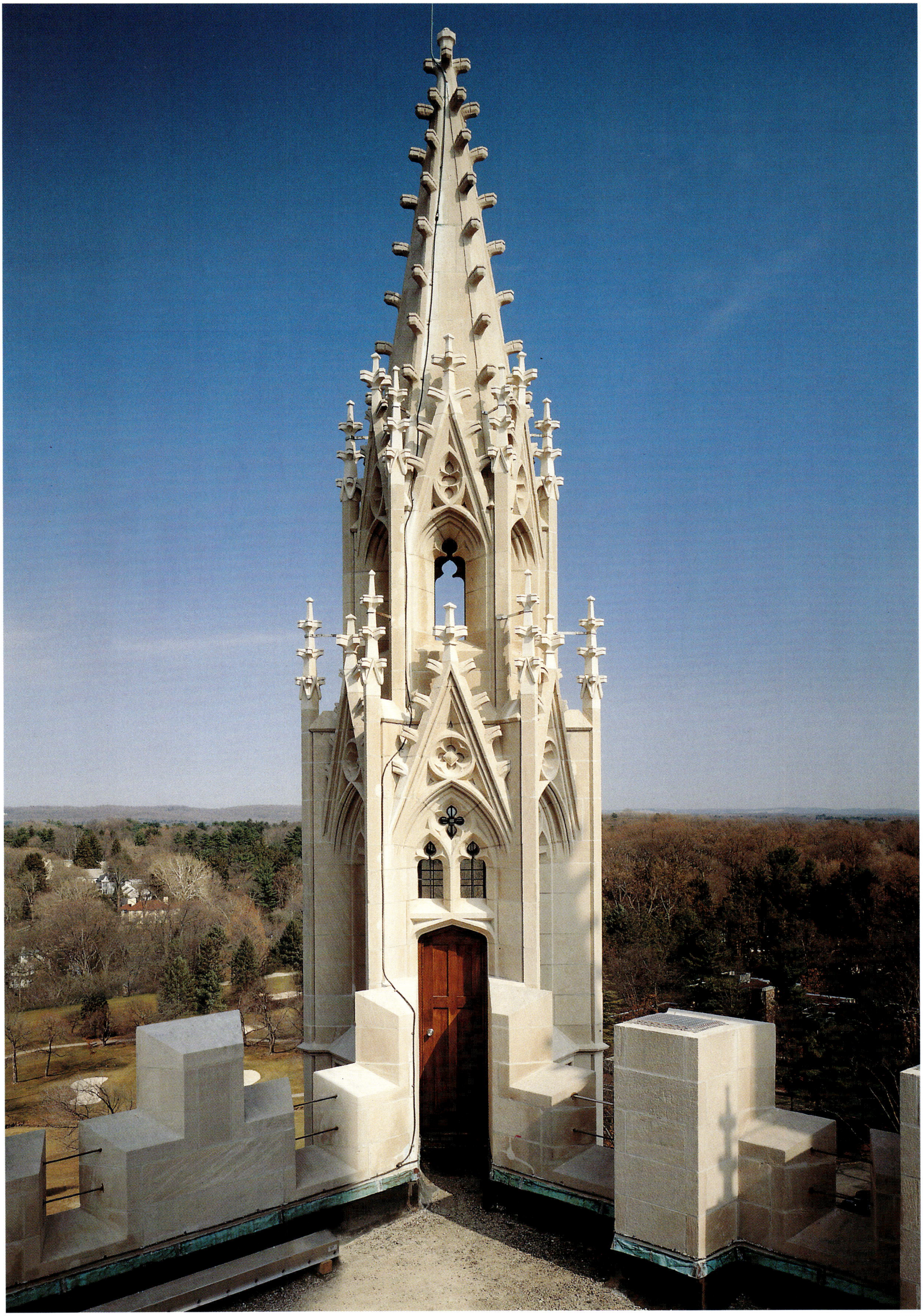

Site plan.

Ground floor plan.

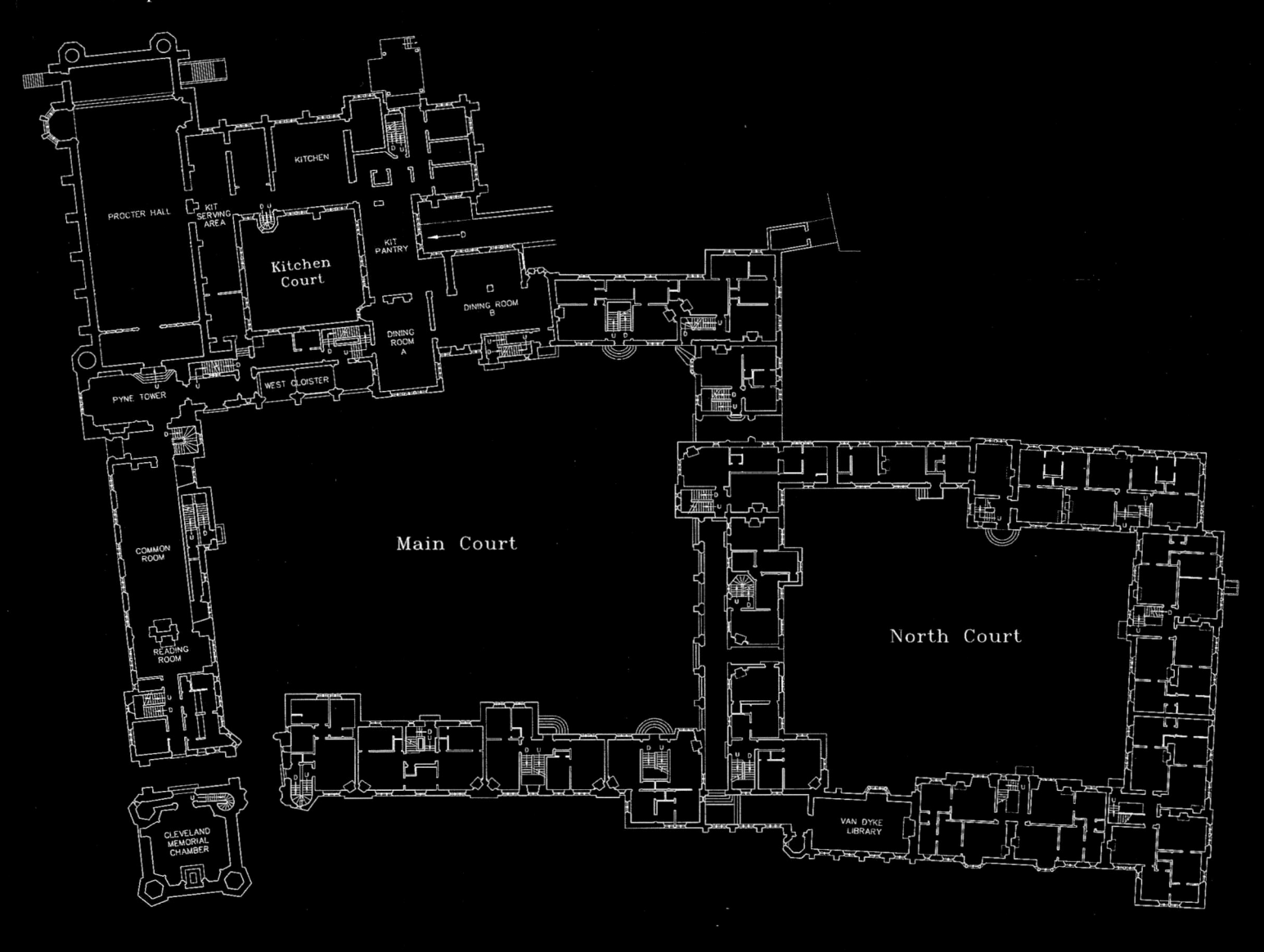

Master's suite.

Van Dyke Library.

Opposite, Cleveland Tower.

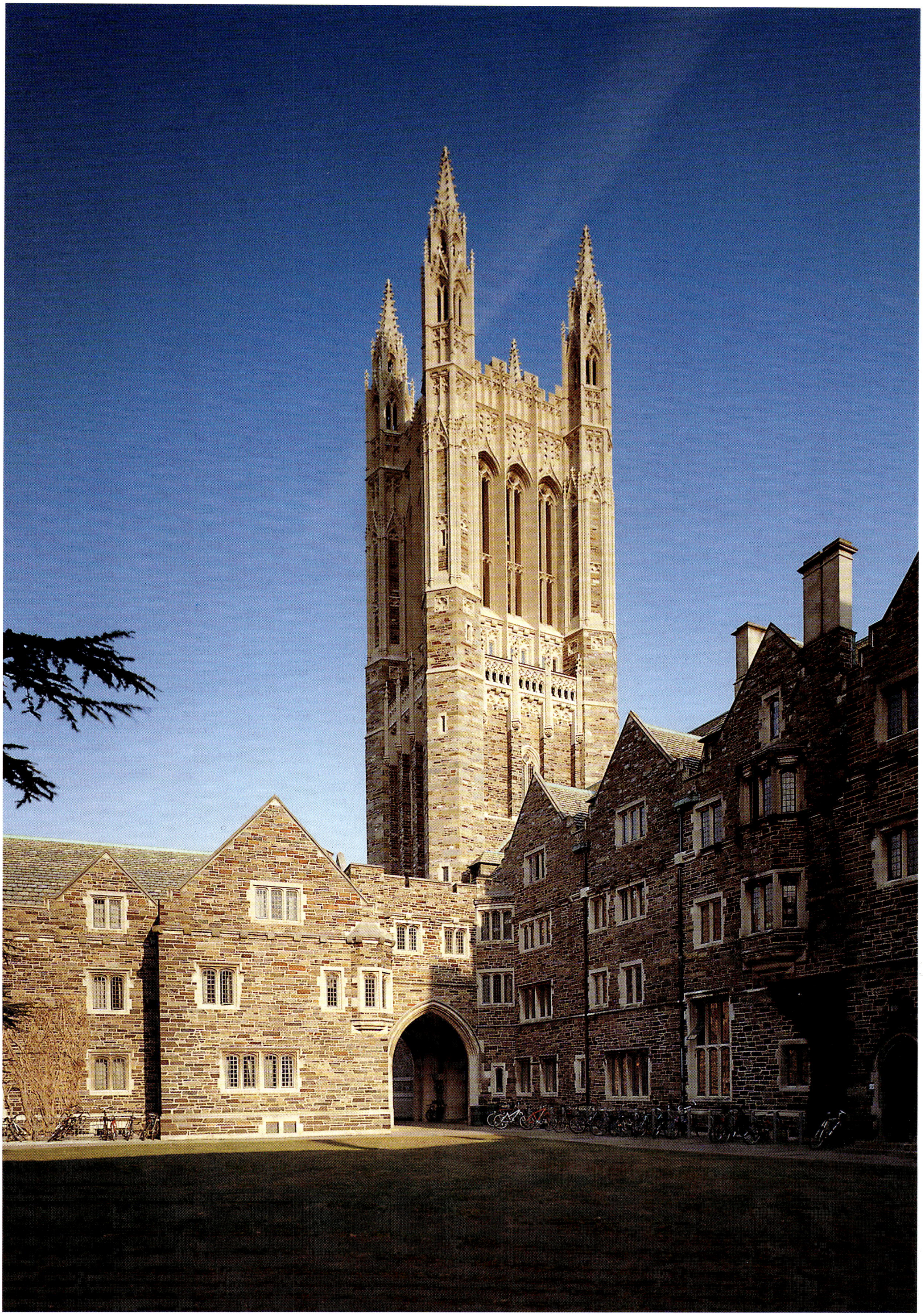

In 1989, the Somerset County Board of Chosen Freeholders began the process of restoring the County's historic 1909 courthouse. While newer facilities, such as a second courthouse and a new administration building, had been built to accommodate the growing County government, the historic courthouse was still the focal point of the complex. Recognizing the symbolic and architectural significance of the building, the Freeholders set a goal of preserving and upgrading the facility to allow greater use of the building and to ensure its survival for future generations.

The restoration of the building, on both the exterior and interior, renewed the significant amount of original building fabric that was still in place. On the exterior, the marble was carefully cleaned and repaired. The front steps were dismantled and rebuilt to correct structural damage and settlement problems. The marble parapet was dismantled, repaired, and reassembled with a new stainless steel bracing system incorporated to meet the seismic code. All of the original windows were removed, repaired, and reinstalled with new integral weatherstripping. The roof was replaced with new standing seam, terne-coated stainless steel. The focal point of the exterior is the cupola, surmounted by a figure of Justice, which was restored to its original appearance.

On the interior, restoration work focused on the primary public spaces: the entry vestibules, the rotunda, and the main courtroom. The rotunda has traditionally functioned as the primary gathering space in the building, and its three-story space visually connects all of the floors of the building. Retaining the open space and the two adjacent open stairs required the insertion of a smoke evacuation system and sprinklers; grillework and sprinkler heads were carefully located to minimize their visual impact. An elevator and new bathrooms were added in unobtrusive locations to make the building fully accessible to persons with disabilities.

The main courtroom required modifications for comfort and continuing use. Sprinklers, improved air circulation and life safety devices were all carefully inserted. The room had suffered acoustical problems since the building opened, and attempts to rectify the problems had resulted in a variety of applied acoustical treatments. These were removed and a monolithic, tinted acoustical material applied to cover wall and ceiling surfaces, resulting in good acoustical performance with no negative impact to the integrity of the room. Key decorative finishes included the marble floors and wainscot, wood trim, *scagliola* columns, brass light fixtures and stained glass ceiling panel, all of which were cleaned, repaired, and refinished.

A subsequent project involving the restoration of the marble and granite Lord Memorial Fountain, a Neoclassical site feature designed by John Russell Pope in 1909-1910, was completed in the summer of 2000.

Somerville, NJ, 1996

Somerset County Courthouse

Front elevation.

Main courtroom.

Rotunda detail.

Main courtroom from mezzanine.

Opposite, detail of exterior materials.

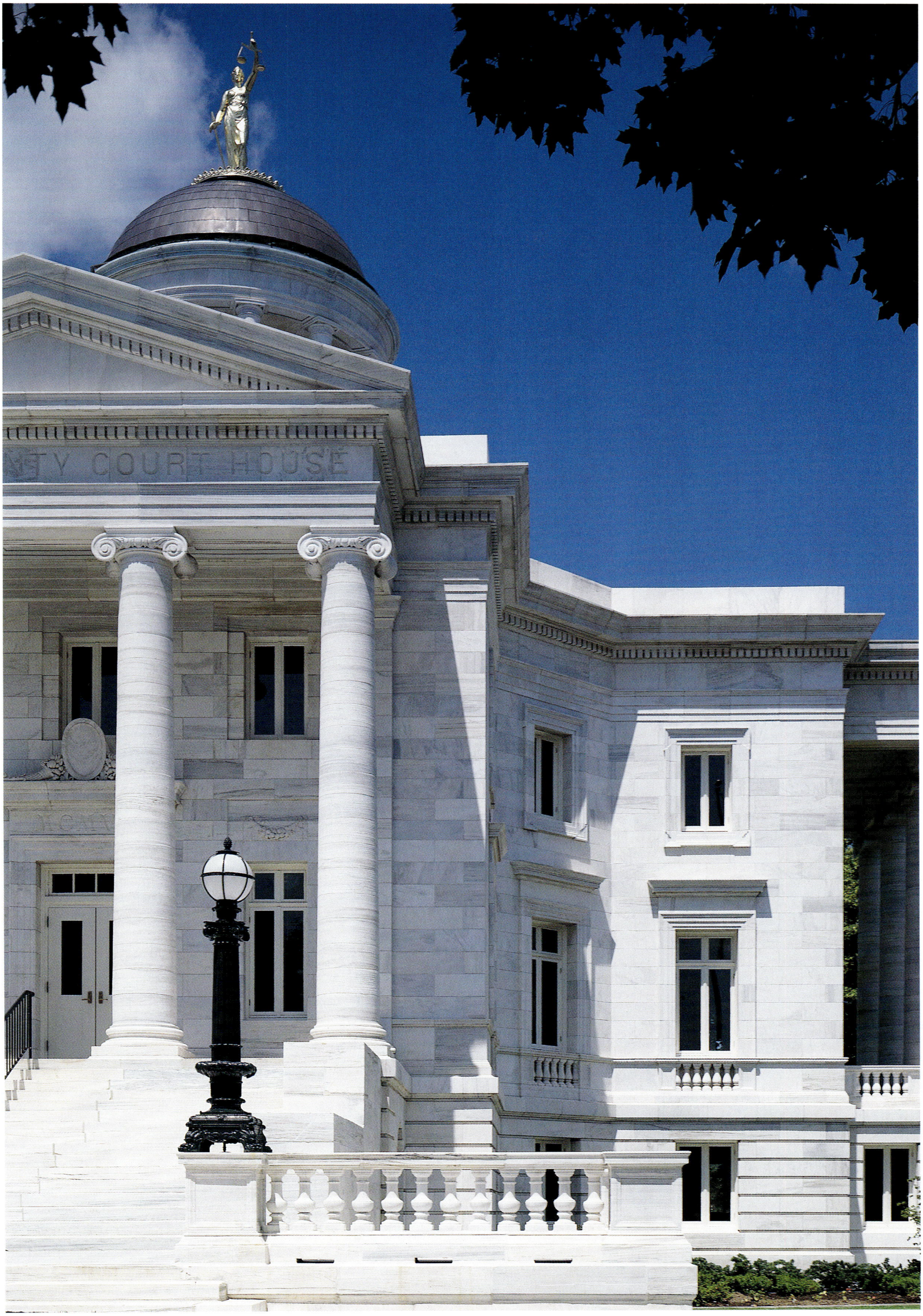
NTY COURT HOUSE

First floor plan.

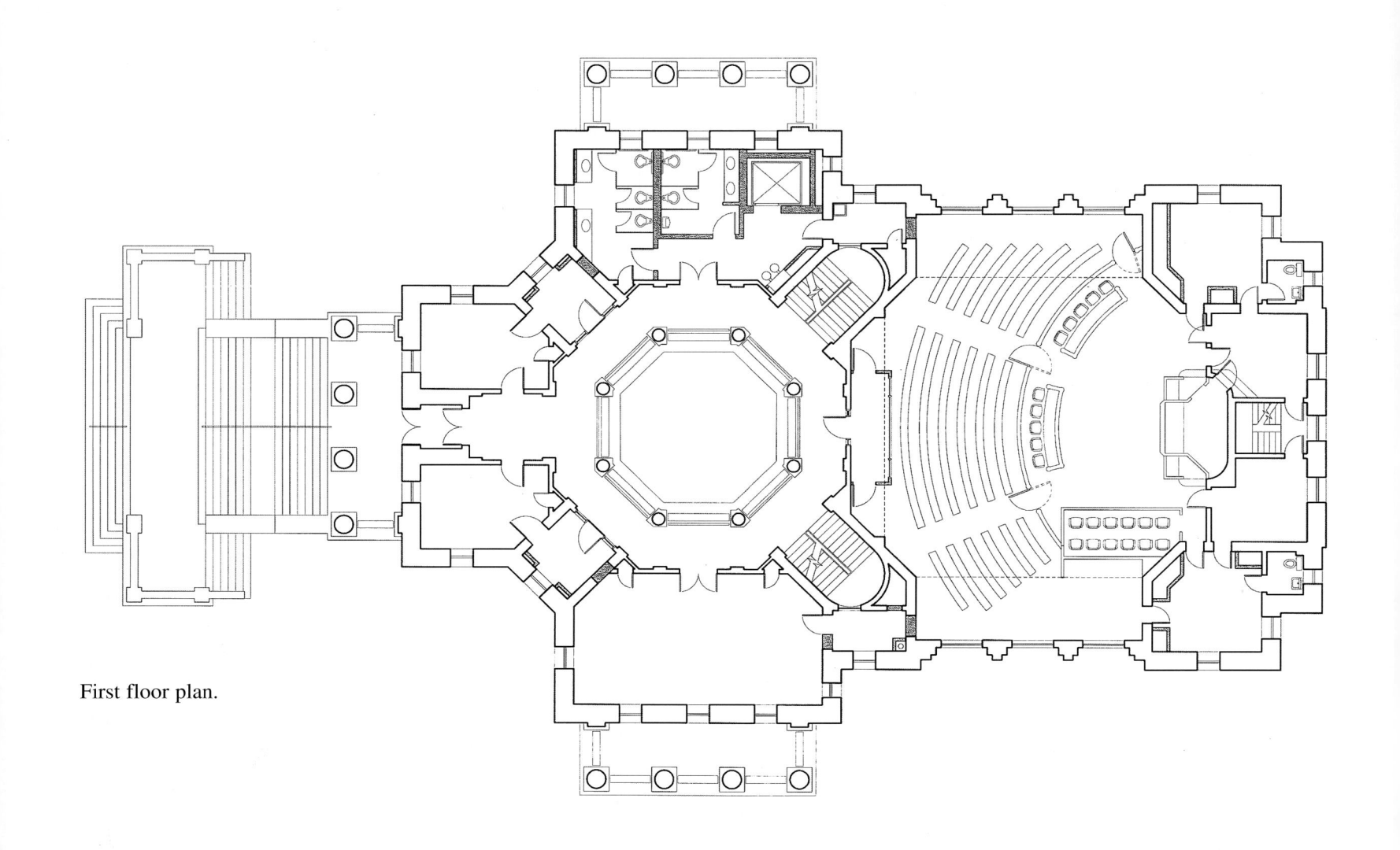

Site plan showing the Courthouse and the Lord Memorial Fountain.

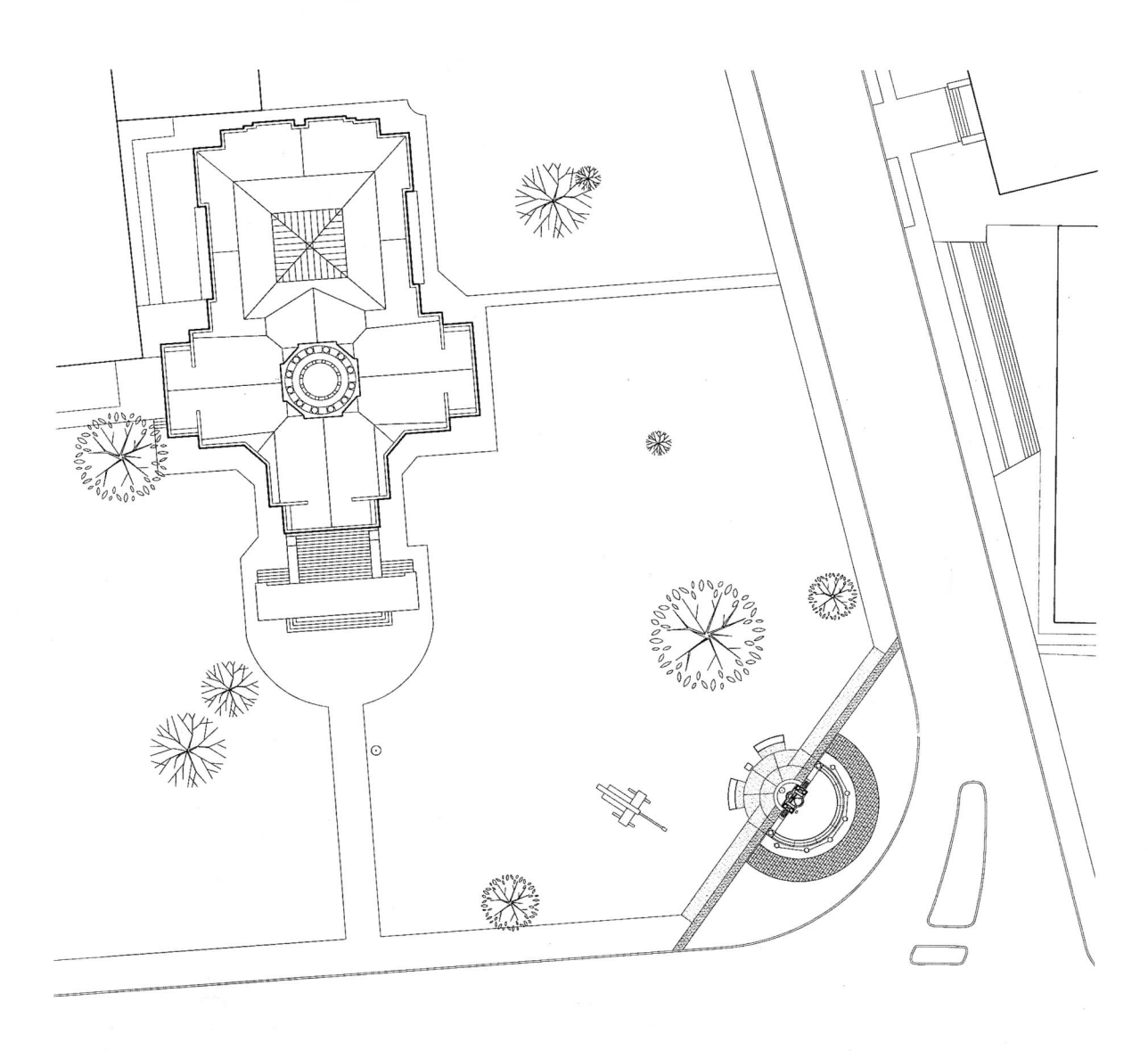

Opposite, Rotunda.

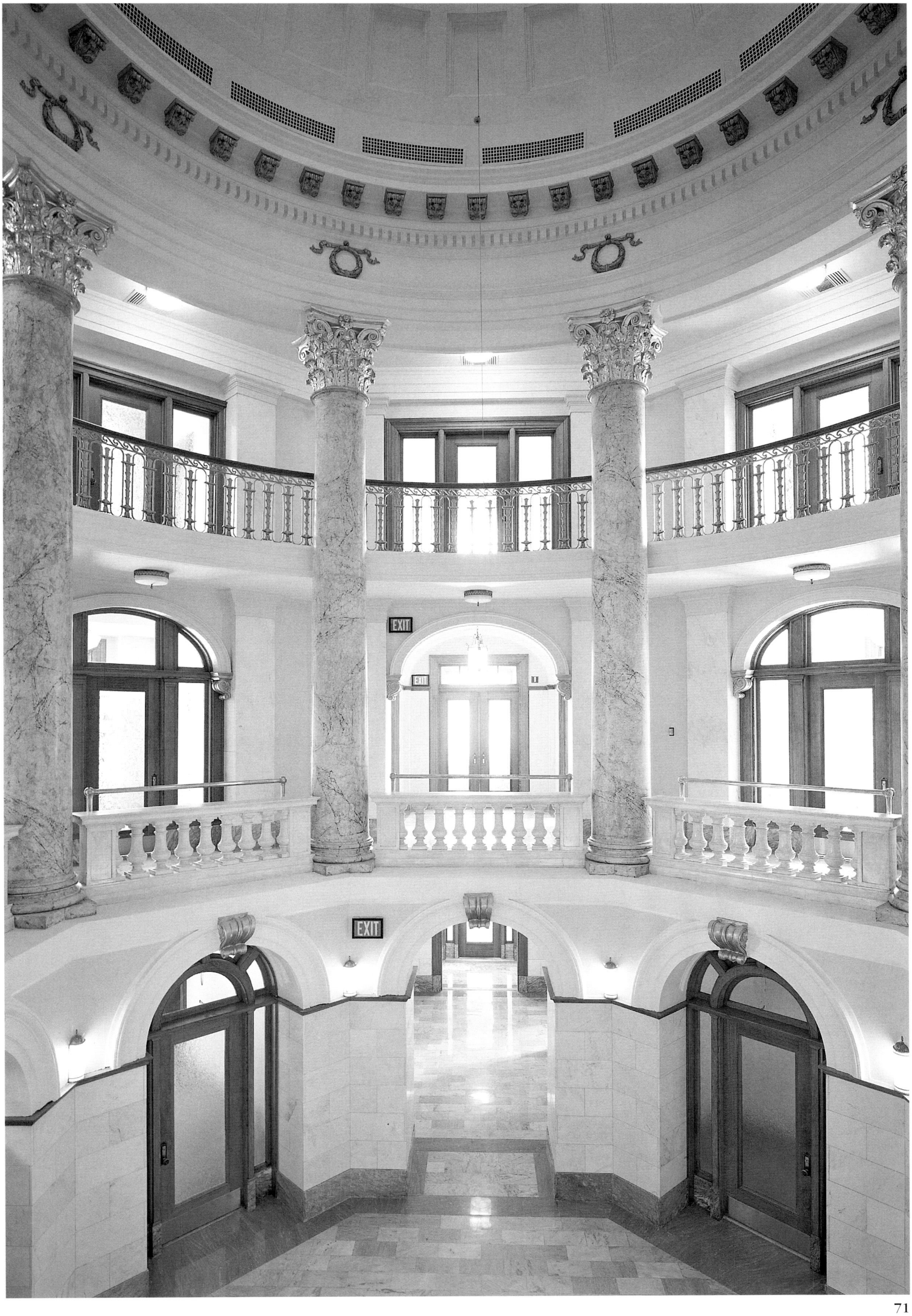
EXIT
EXIT

Lower courtroom.

Dome and oculus.

Opposite, Rotunda, third floor.

Main courtroom facing Judge's Bench.

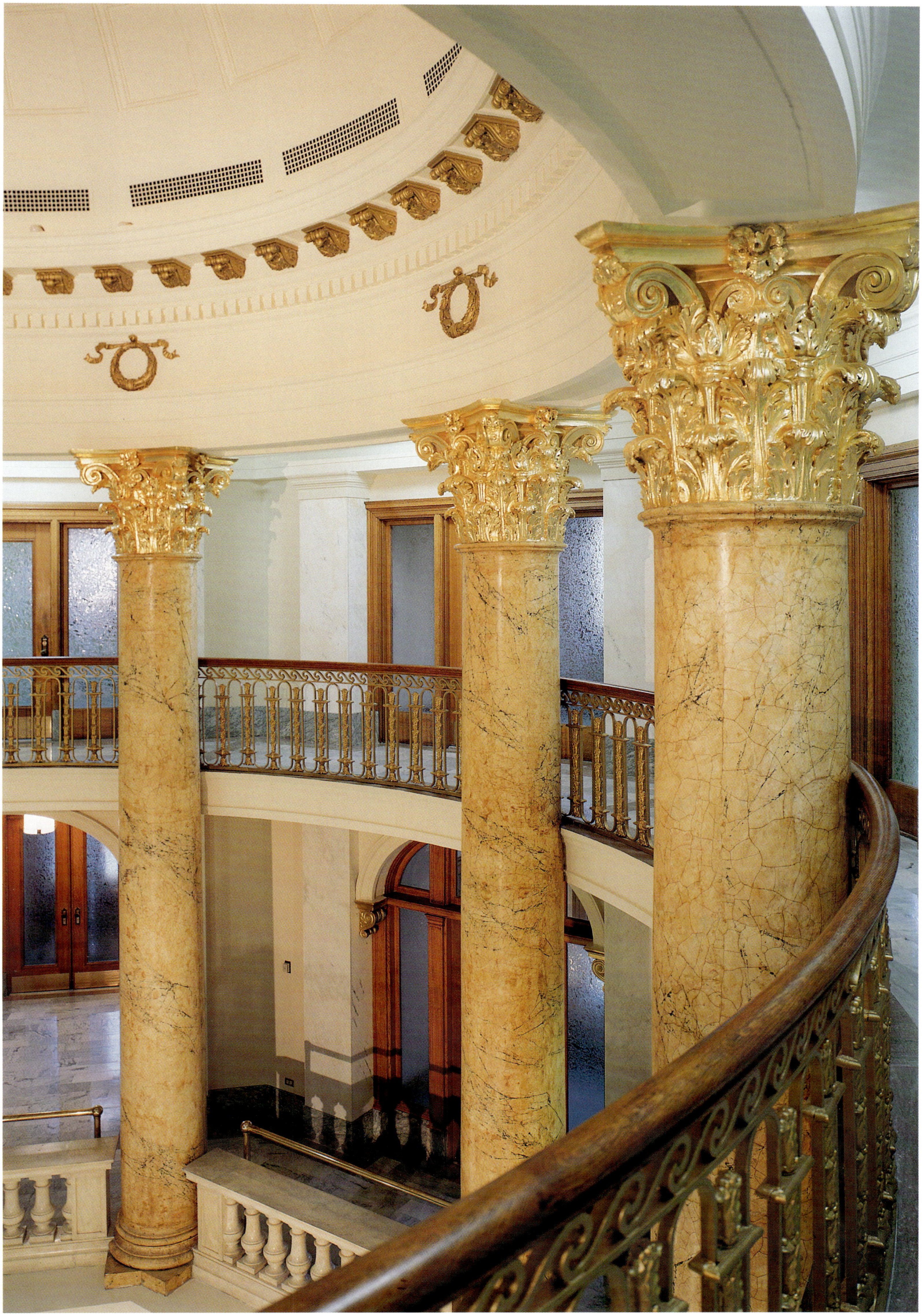

The new family courts building is located at the heart of the downtown. It is one component of a larger public-private redevelopment project that includes a 430-car parking deck and more than 10,000 square feet for the downtown campus of a county college. The building is designed to simultaneously reinforce the existing urban grid and introduce greater building density into an underdeveloped part of the city. In an effort to create a welcoming structure that establishes a dialogue with neighboring buildings, a shallow public zone creates a civic forecourt and smaller bays along the side street relate to the adjacent residential block. A colossal order of Solomonic columns defines the entry and extends the geometry of the interior.

The building comprises 99,000 square feet, and contains a double-height lobby, two large and nine small courtrooms, three hearing rooms, support spaces for judges and staff, private offices, open office areas, conference rooms, and libraries. Specialized program inclusions are waiting areas for children and victims of domestic violence. A partial basement is used for a lunchroom, loading area, storage, and a holding area for detainees. The building has multiple elevators and corridors that separate circulation for the public, prisoners, staff, and judges. The dramatic entry and double-height lobby acknowledge the significance and gravity of the judicial system, while intimate, comfortable spaces inside provide families privacy and a calm environment in which to participate in the difficult business of the family courts.

With an eye to long-term needs, the family courts now occupy three of the four floors and the partial basement; the fourth floor was constructed as shell space for future expansion. The adjacent parking deck was constructed simultaneously and designed in conjunction with the courts building so that the two structures, while not physically connected, relate to each other in appearance.

The building has a structural steel frame with a masonry exterior that is extended into the double-height lobby. The masonry exterior uses two types of pre-cast units: a brown, rusticated stone for the base, and a smooth, paler stone for the walls above to evoke the limestone traditionally used for monumental civic buildings. Cast stone is used to trim the base. The cornice is constructed of steel and aluminum and the windows are framed in aluminum. Inside, the lobby walls and monumental stair are of pre-cast masonry and the floor is terrazzo. Etched glass interior windows, installed in niches over the grand stair, are backlit to provide a soft illumination. The courtrooms and judges' chambers feature custom cherry millwork.

New Brunswick, NJ, 1990

Civic Square III:
Middlesex County Courthouse

Front view.

Lobby.

Site plan.

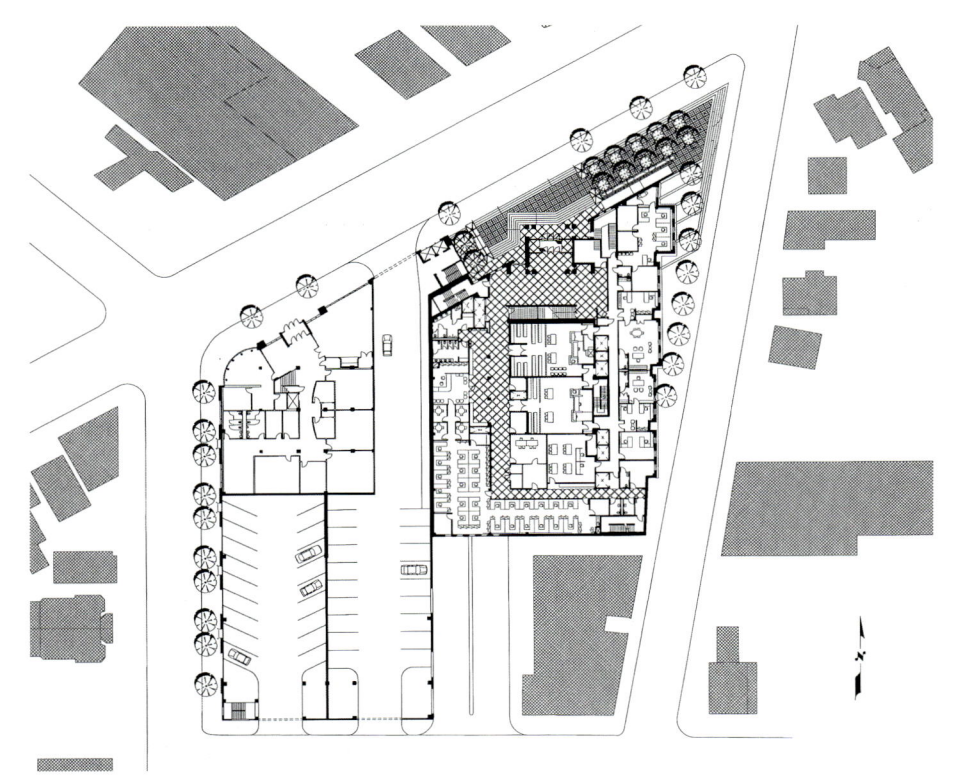

Second floor plan.

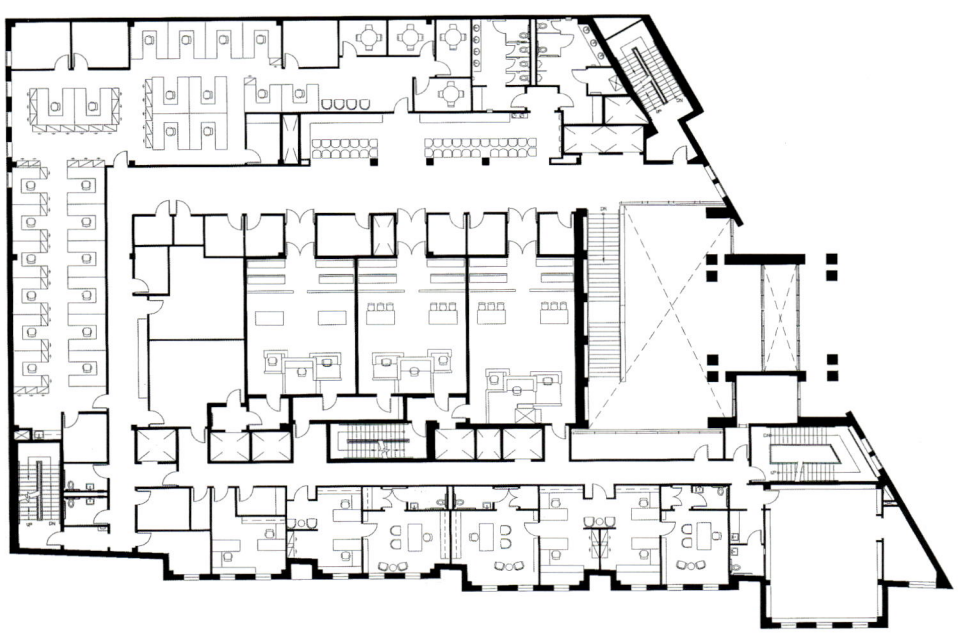

Entry detail.

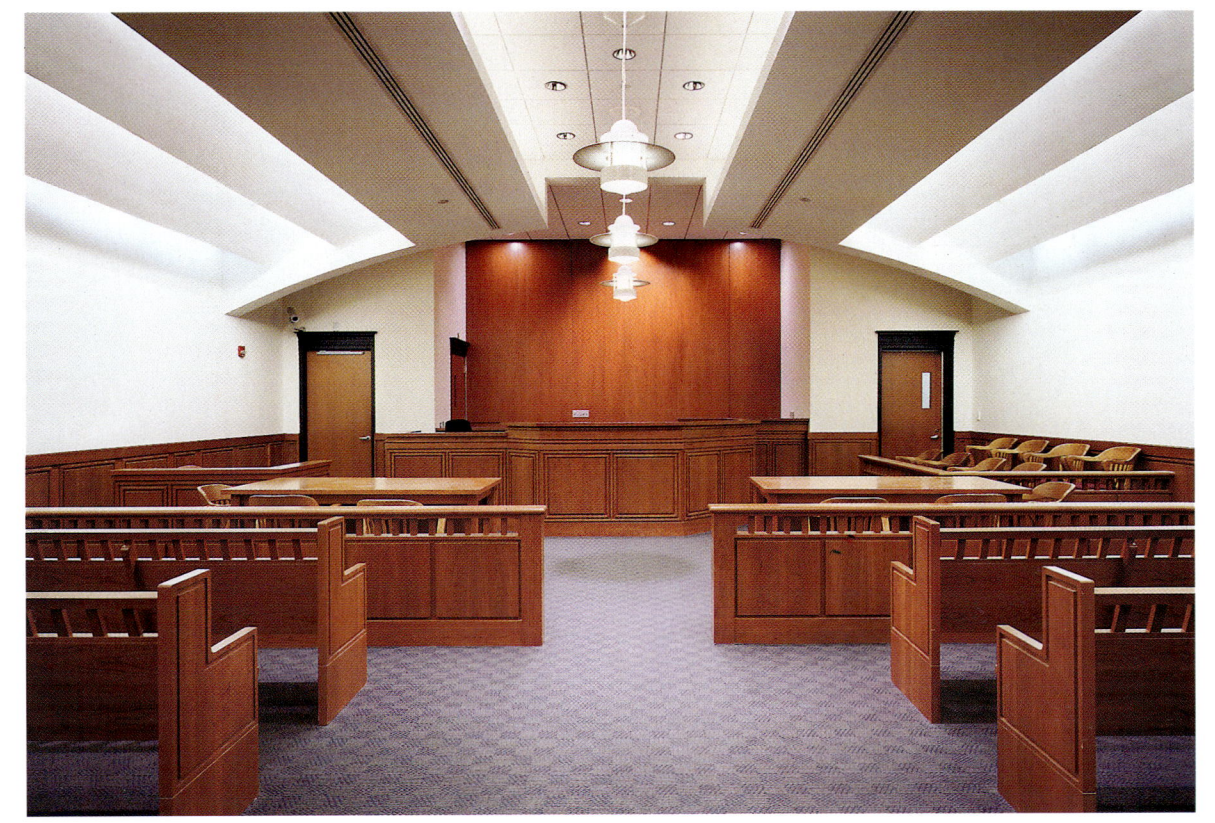

Courtroom.

Wood Works

The Princeton Child Development Institute is an internationally recognized institution that specializes in the treatment of autistic children, trains educators, and supports a research facility. With the school's expansion in to a young adult program, twelve thousand square feet of new space were required. Programming needs included classroom space, a multipurpose room, a training kitchen, staff workroom, administrative space, conference room and other support space.

The complex is located in a flat agrarian landscape flanked by an orchard and farm. Prior to receiving its new addition, the facility comprised shed-roofed volumes rotated forty-five degrees from the road, and seemed to be disconnected from its context. The goal in this project was to create more natural and contextual relationships between building and landscape, just as the mission of the school is the integration of its students into a more normalized social environment.

The addition is configured as two flanking volumes, satisfying internal needs for program distribution with an administration wing on the north side and the new young adult program on the south side. The division of the additions allows the new building to embrace the old, giving the school a new visual identity while retaining all of its original core. In plan geometry and massing, the new building contrasts with the original, energizing the entire composition.

Spines within the additions clarify internal circulation. Major and minor rooms adjoin these corridors and connect to the existing circulation system to achieve a new flow pattern. The spines are given an external expression that relates to the agrarian architecture of the region. Major spaces such as the conference room, multipurpose room and staff room are high, clerestory-lit spaces which take advantage of views of the landscape. In general, interiors have been carefully lighted and arranged to foster the kind of supportive atmosphere that has led to dramatic success in this program.

Lawrence Township, NJ,
1996

Princeton Child Development Institute

View of entry.

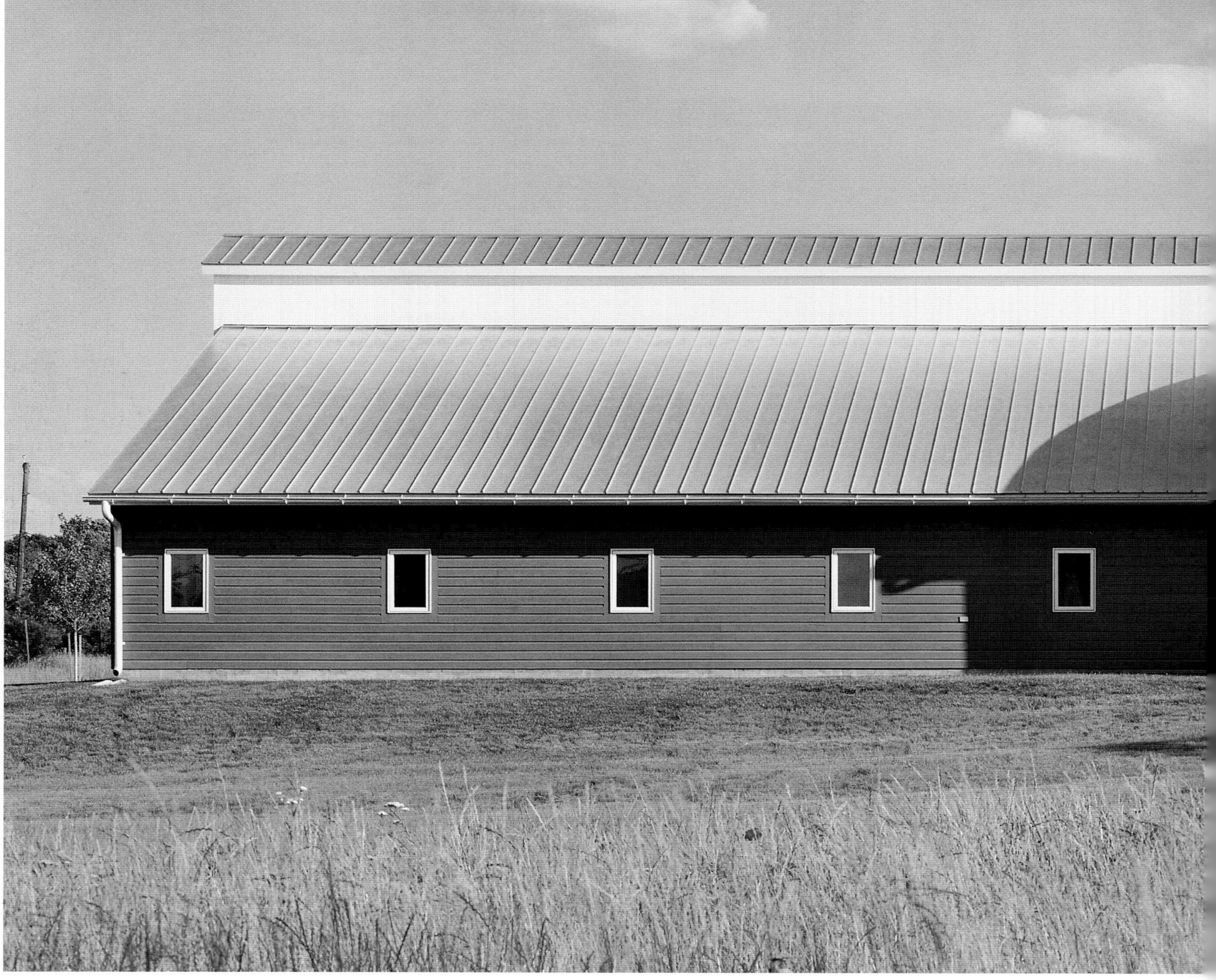

View of new facade.

Entry.

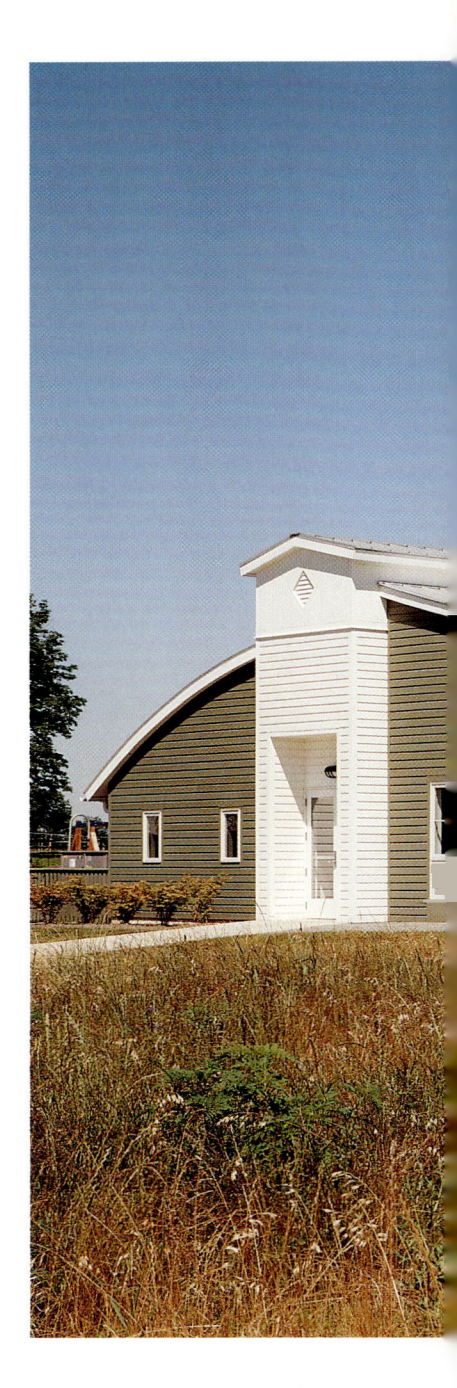

Multipurpose Room.

View of rear addition.

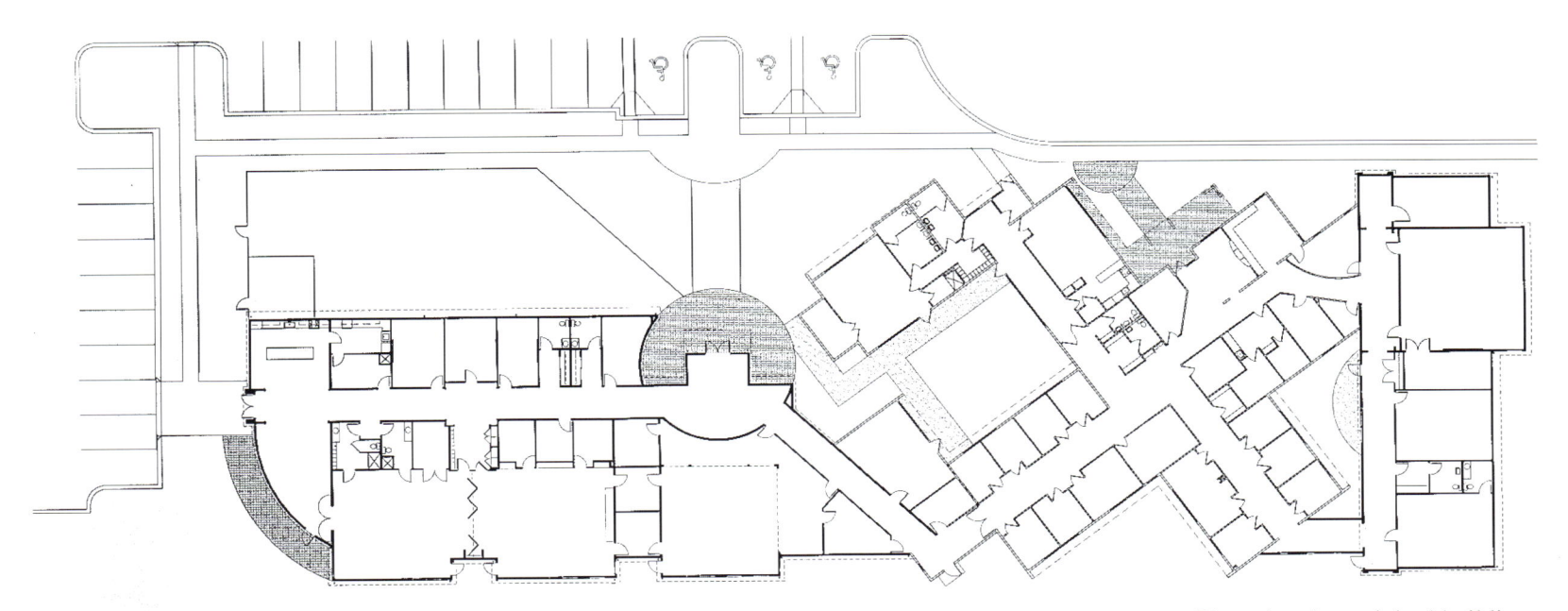

Plan showing original building and front and back additions.

85

The new headquarters for the New Jersey Housing & Mortgage Finance Agency is located in the former wire rope fabrication building of the prominent John A. Roebling's Sons Company in Trenton. The project had a number of significant economic and social goals. Primarily, it represented the agency's commitment to keeping the workforce in the city and their contribution to a significant adaptive use project. The organization of the plan on an urban model gives coherence to the agency for employees and visitors and expresses the fundamental mandate of this agency, which is, through economic development, to support the construction needs of the state housing industry.

The one-story building is a broad, top-lighted space with a 50-foot tall former testing room at its entry. The interior plan links four major squares. These "urban centers" are distinct departmental addresses, including administration, executive, finance, and single-family housing. Each center is different in character and materials and related to activities of the department. Single-family, for instance, is defined by a wood pavilion at the center which is house-like in character. The executive department, near the entry, is a gearlike structure reflecting the dynamism of both the original plant and the new agency.

The entry, through the high bay testing building, is the location of a gallery, reception and meeting spaces. To preserve the interior character of this space, the new elements are constructed within a volume treated as a box within a box. Materials and color contrast with the red brick exterior. The outer space functions as a gallery, display, and library room.

Trenton, NJ, 1995

New Jersey Housing & Mortgage Finance Agency

Front elevation of the exhibition space.

Administrative area.

Board room.

Opposite page, executive area.

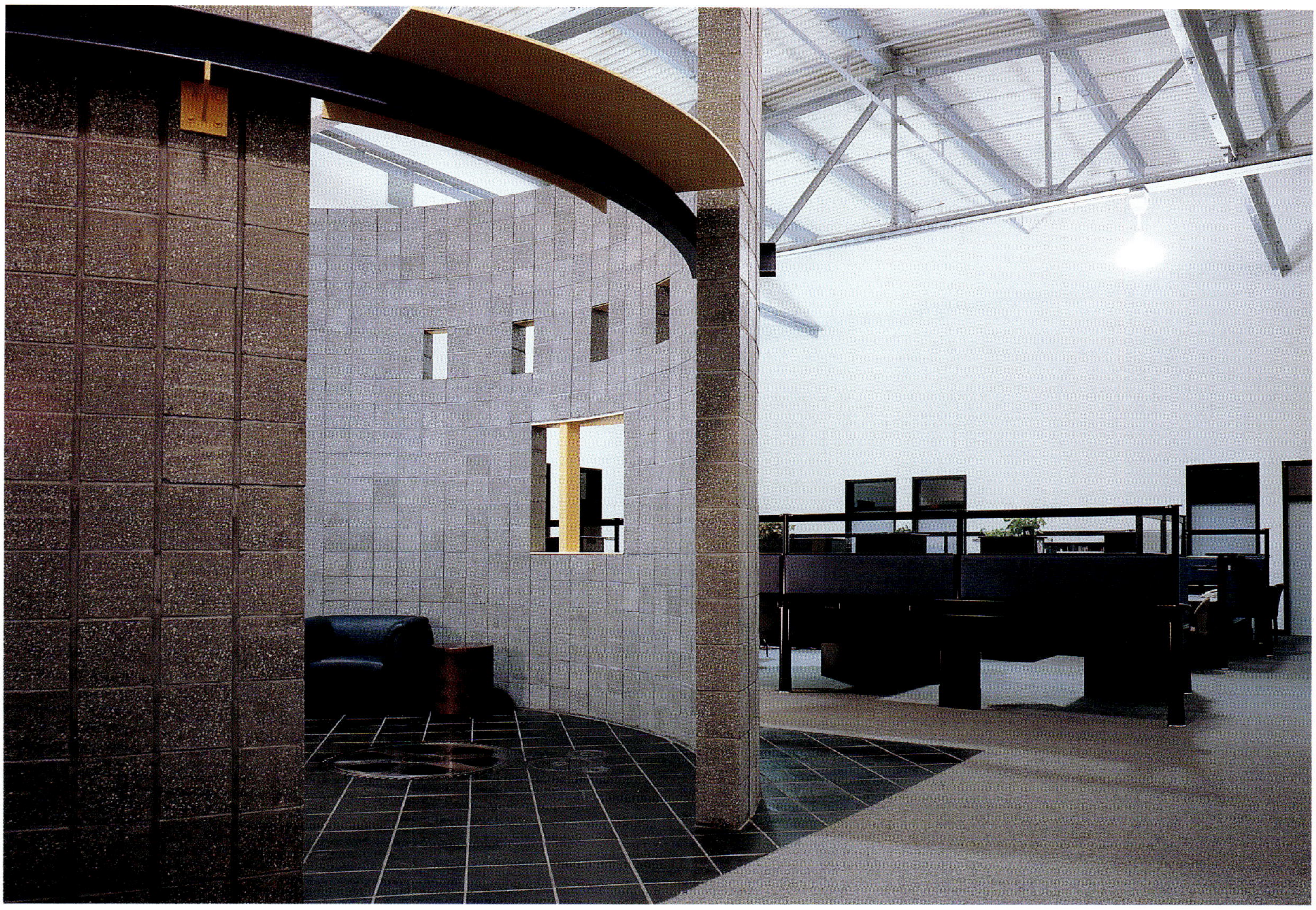

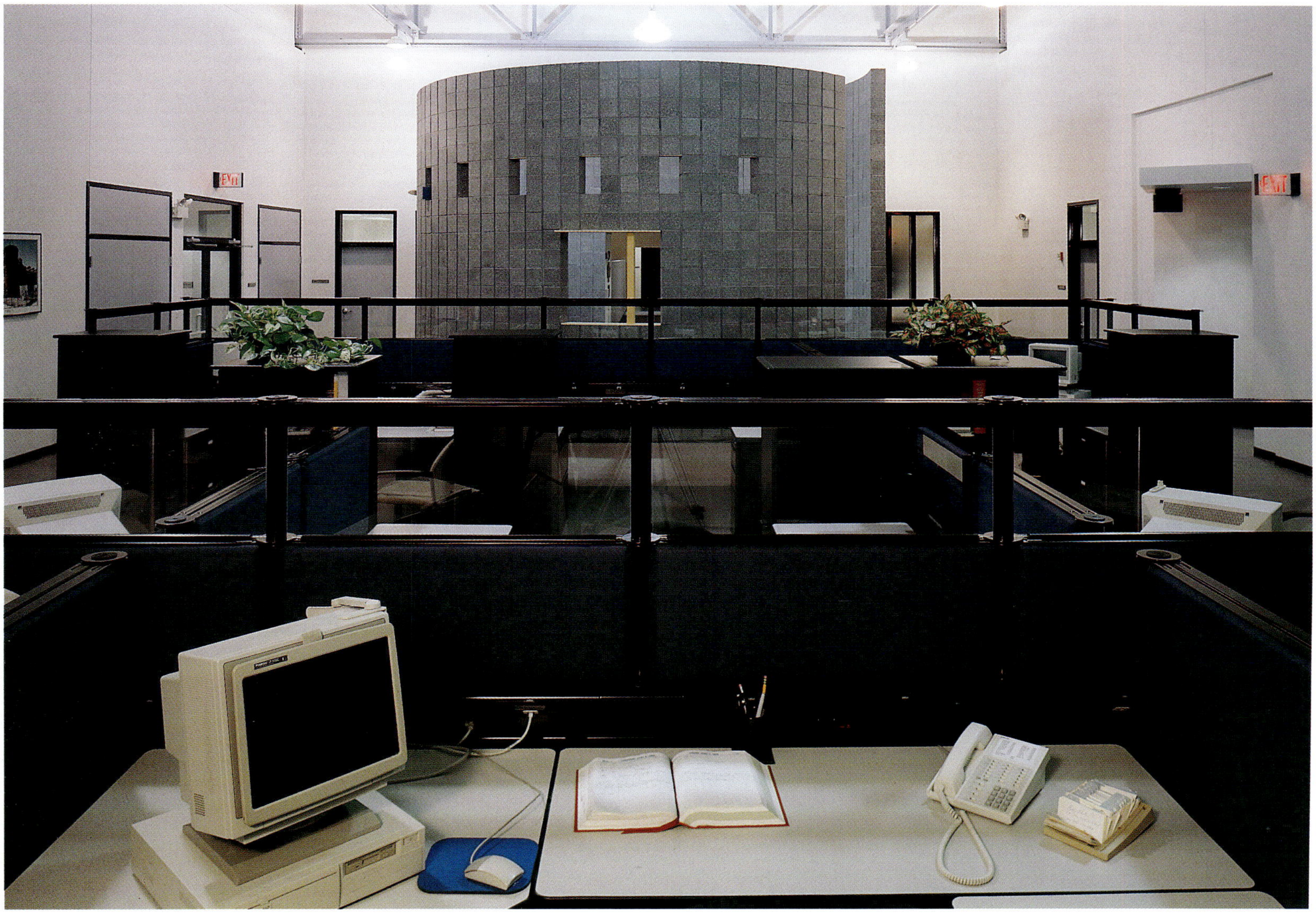

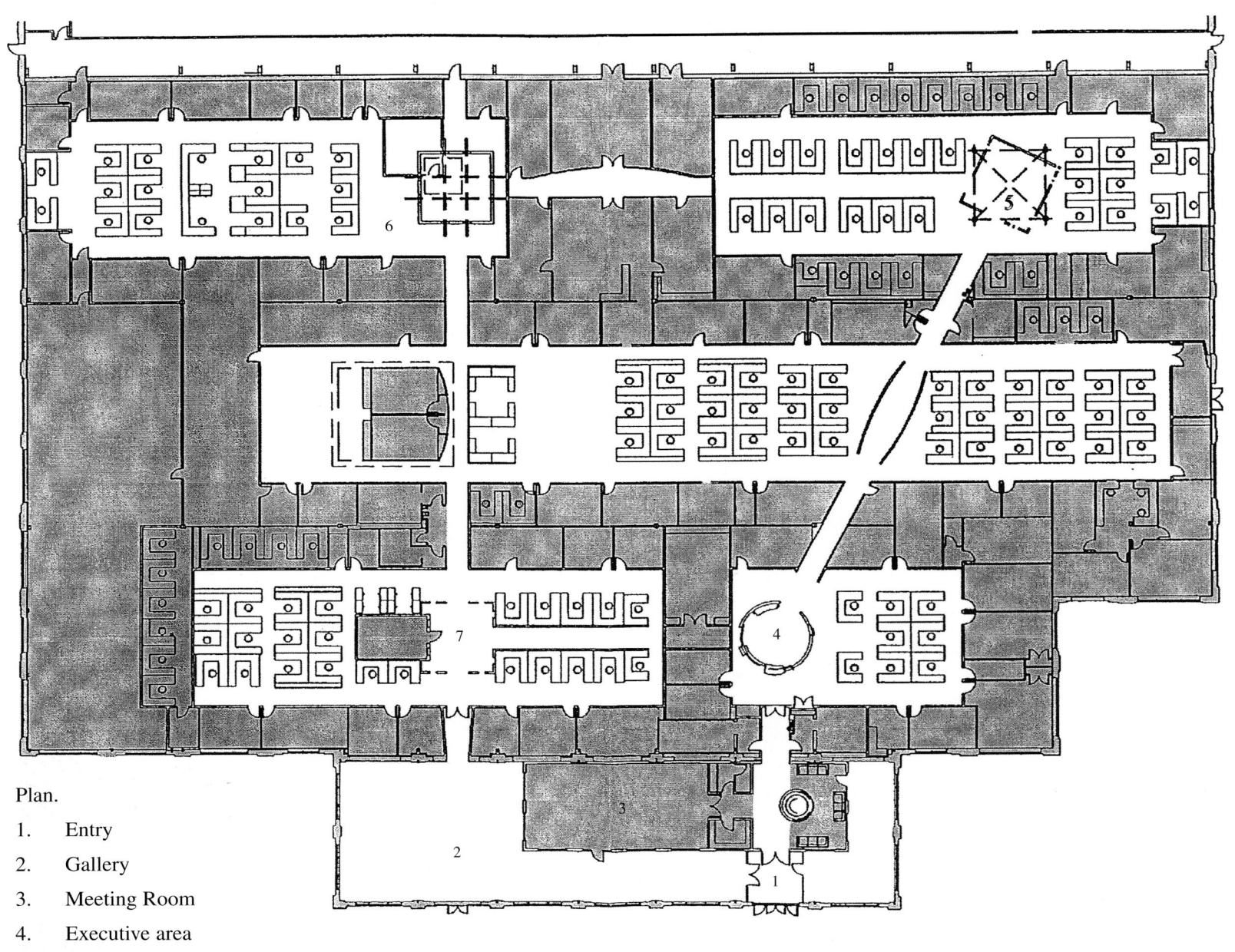

Plan.
1. Entry
2. Gallery
3. Meeting Room
4. Executive area
5. Single-family housing
6. Administration
7. Finance

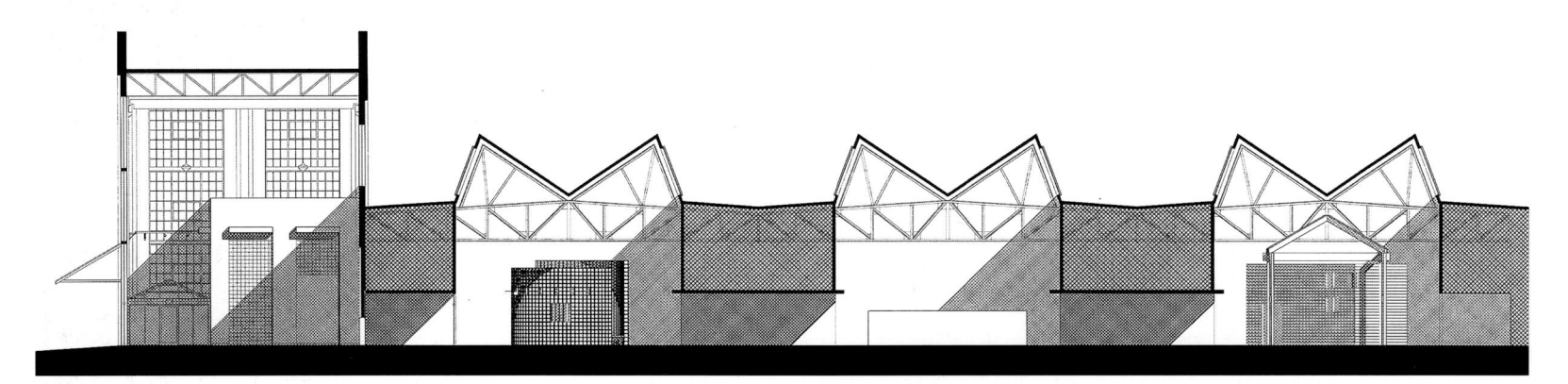

Section.

Finance area.

Single-family housing.   Administration.

The University Cottage Club, originally completed in 1906, was designed by Charles McKim of McKim Mead and White, the pre-eminent architectural firm of the turn of the last century. Among University Cottage Club's noteworthy features is the oak woodwork in its impressive library, which is modeled after the library at Oxford University's Merton College. As at Merton, the focal point of the Cottage Club library is a classical screen dividing the writing room from the main library space.

The restoration of the oak-paneled library in the University Cottage Club is but one phase of an extensive and ongoing restoration project at the building. Initially, in 1984, the firm prepared a comprehensive preservation plan that included recommendations for major interior restorations in the library, dining room and gallery; restoration of the brick and marble exterior facades and wood elements such as the cornice and colonnade; replacement of the slate and copper roof; a new fire suppression system; upgrades to the building's systems to bring the structure into compliance with current life-safety codes and accessibility guidelines; and landscape improvements.
The preservation plan continues to be implemented in stages to enable the building to remain in use during the renovations.

The restoration of the library required careful study and the preparation of test samples by an architectural conservator. Based on information revealed in this process, methods were specified for removal of inappropriate finishes, for repair and restoration of woodwork, and for application of new finishes. The project involved dismantling the oak casework and sections of the oak flooring to facilitate replacement of the electrical system. Chandeliers and sconces were removed from the room and restored off-site while the paneling, ceiling, and carved elements were repaired and refinished. Finally, the cases were reinstalled and refinished to match the other wood features, and the light fixtures were reinstalled and relamped. The result of the work was the re-creation of the form, materials and richness of McKim's landmark design.

Princeton, NJ, 1992

University Cottage Club Library

Front elevation.

Writing room.

Floor plans.
1. Dining Room
2. Breakfast Room
3. Kitchen
4. Portico
5. Court
6. Gallery
7. Hall
8. Vestibule
9. Red Room
10. Palmer Room
11. Stairhall
12. Lounge
13. Bedroom
14. Office
15. Billiard Room
16. Writing Room
17. Library

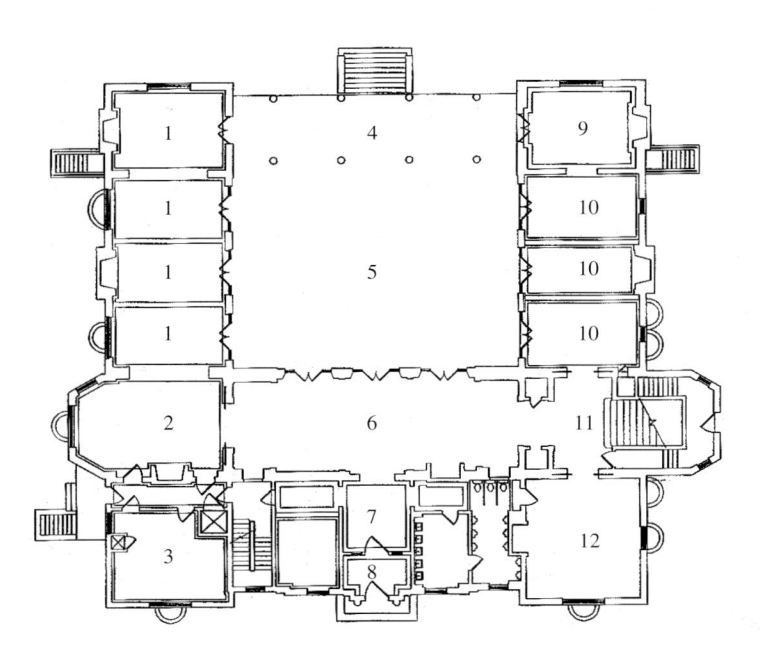

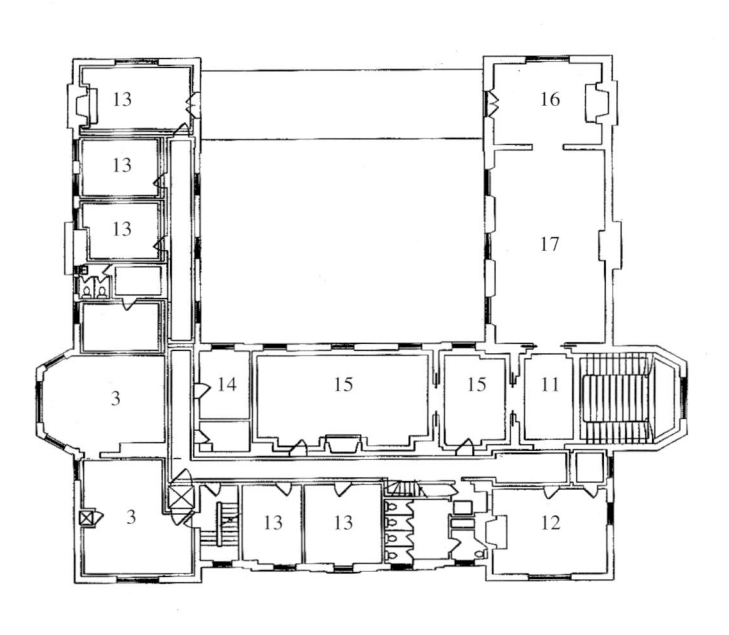

Library.

Rear elevation.

Stucco Works

The program for Pool and Pool House I consists of a changing room, an equipment room, storage space, a place sheltered from direct sunlight, and the pool itself. To heighten the physical sensation of immersion in water, the program is accommodated within a structure that mirrors the excavated void of the pool.

One passes through this architectural space in ritualistic preparation for entering the pool. Sensations of sound, of direct and reflected light, of warmth and coolness are accentuated by the configuration of the structure and the use of elemental materials.

The stage-like aperture at the center of composition frames human form in the landscape, and orchestrates the changing effects of light and shade.

Far Hills, NJ, 1991

Pool and Pool House I

View from house.

Interior views.

Site plan.

View toward house.

101

Night view.

Section.

Midday view.

West elevation.

The Casino Building, a 60,000 square foot building, was designed by Bruce Price in the late 1890s for George Gould, son of financier Jay Gould. The Casino dominated the expansive Gould Estate, and was conceived as a "palace of entertainment" that included an indoor polo field; a swimming pool; court tennis, squash and racquets courts; a bowling alley; a ballroom; and thirty-two guest rooms. In the 1920s, The Sisters of Mercy of New Jersey acquired the entire Gould Estate for use as a college campus. The Casino has been altered little over time, and was listed on the State and National Registers of Historic Places in addition to being designated a National Historic Landmark.

In 1995, the firm prepared measured drawings and a preservation plan for the Casino to serve as the basis for a renovation of the building to meet the college's current athletic requirements. In 1996, the firm helped the college prepare a successful grant application to the New Jersey Historic Trust. The college has used those monies toward the first phase of the renovation project, which included replacement of all standing seam and flat built-up roofs; replacement of skylights at the court tennis and squash courts; reconstruction and repair of the masonry parapets; conservation of two terra cotta murals over major entrances; restoration of stucco; exiting and fire safety improvements; and improvements to the performance stage located in the original indoor polo field, now used as the field house and auditorium.

The terra cotta bas reliefs over the main entrance depict allegorical scenes with horses, and serve as a fitting preamble for the pageantry of the interior spaces beyond. Where sculptural elements were missing, new ones were made to re-establish the artistic integrity of each mural. The losses of glaze were retouched with new glaze to match the color and texture of the original.

Lakewood, NJ, 1996

Casino Building at Georgian Court College

Elevation showing
reconstructed porch.

Restored porch.

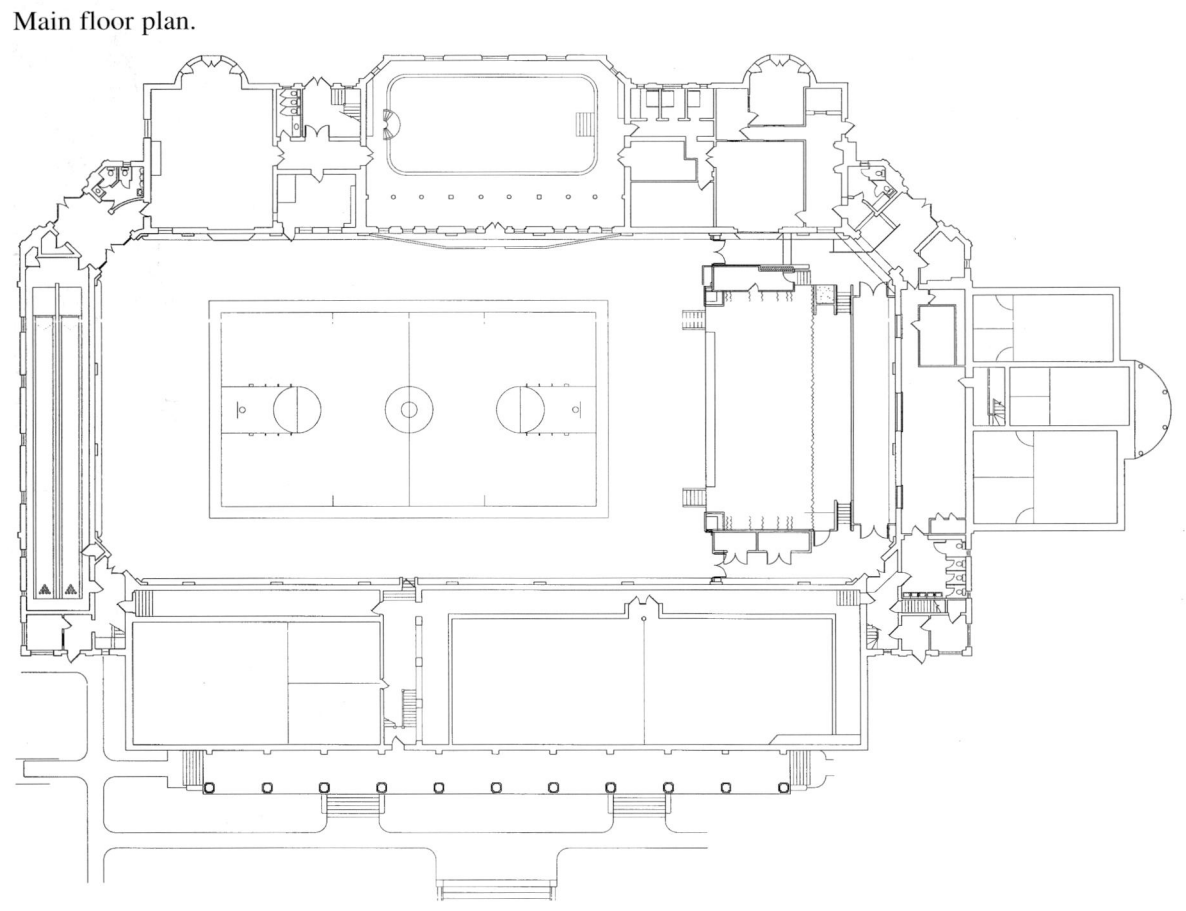

Main floor plan.

Restored arched entrance and
sculptural ornament.

The original 1940s school was configured as a series of parallel building ranges and located on an undulating, rural site adjacent to an active highway. Playing fields surrounded the school. Materials utilized included exposed concrete block and wood strip windows with low sloped roofs.

The new two-story addition faces west with an entrance court arranged around a mature oak tree on the south side. To take advantage of both views of the hilly landscape and outdoor teaching and recreational needs, the addition is "L" shaped in plan with a portal and stair connecting to an upper level. The new wing is configured to give the Upper School a clear identity while linking the two ranges of the existing building in an accessible internal circulation pattern. The front yard, containing parking and drop-off loop, has been reconfigured to provide a safer and more efficient circulation pattern with a new front lobby.

The addition comprises six new classrooms accommodating up to fifteen students each, a computer instruction laboratory and research center, and central gathering space with support services. Renovation of the existing building included achieving full accessibility and larger classrooms.

A semicircular banking of the site around the west facade provides an amphitheater. This arc is extended into the major volume of the interior, a double-height gathering space with an open stair and stepped seating. This space, lighted by a roof monitor, gives access to the classrooms on both levels. The rooms, entered through a thick wall of wood lockers, are screened by an exterior louver system that controls natural light.

Far Hills, NJ, 1997

Far Hills Country Day School

Amphitheatre elevation.

Elevation of classrooms.

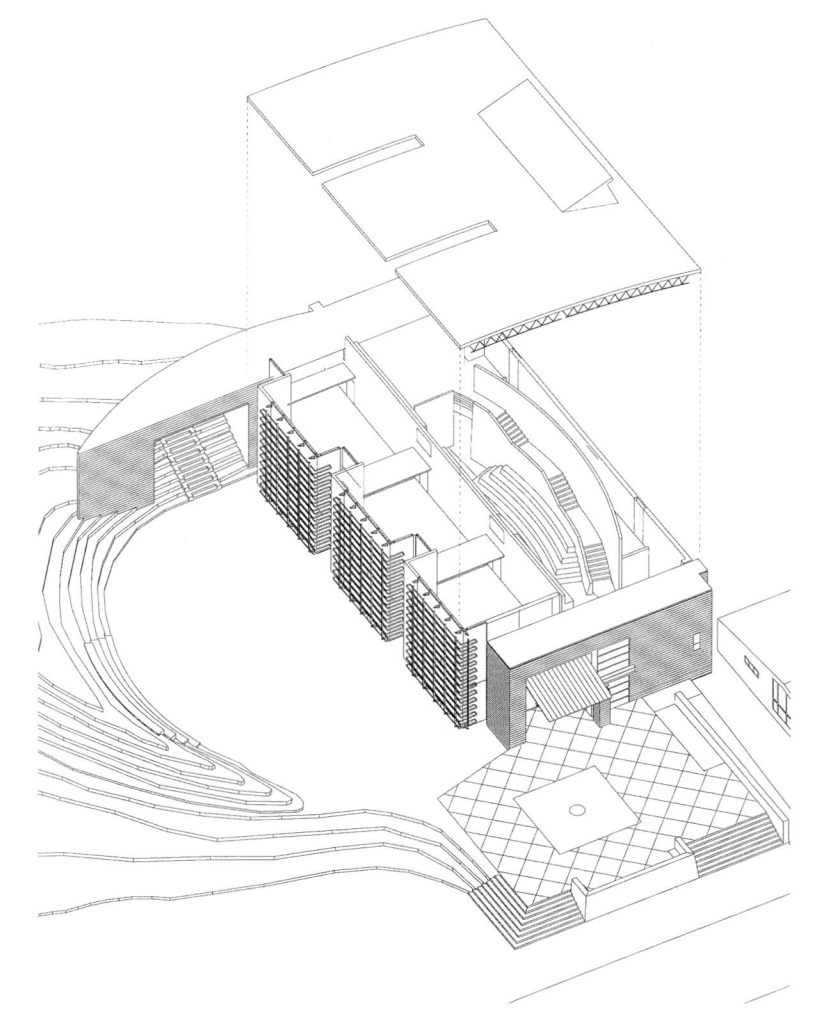

Exploded axonometric.

First floor plan.

1. Terrace
2. Commons
3. Classroom
4. Computer Center
5. Amphitheatre
6. Upper Level
7. Mechanical Room

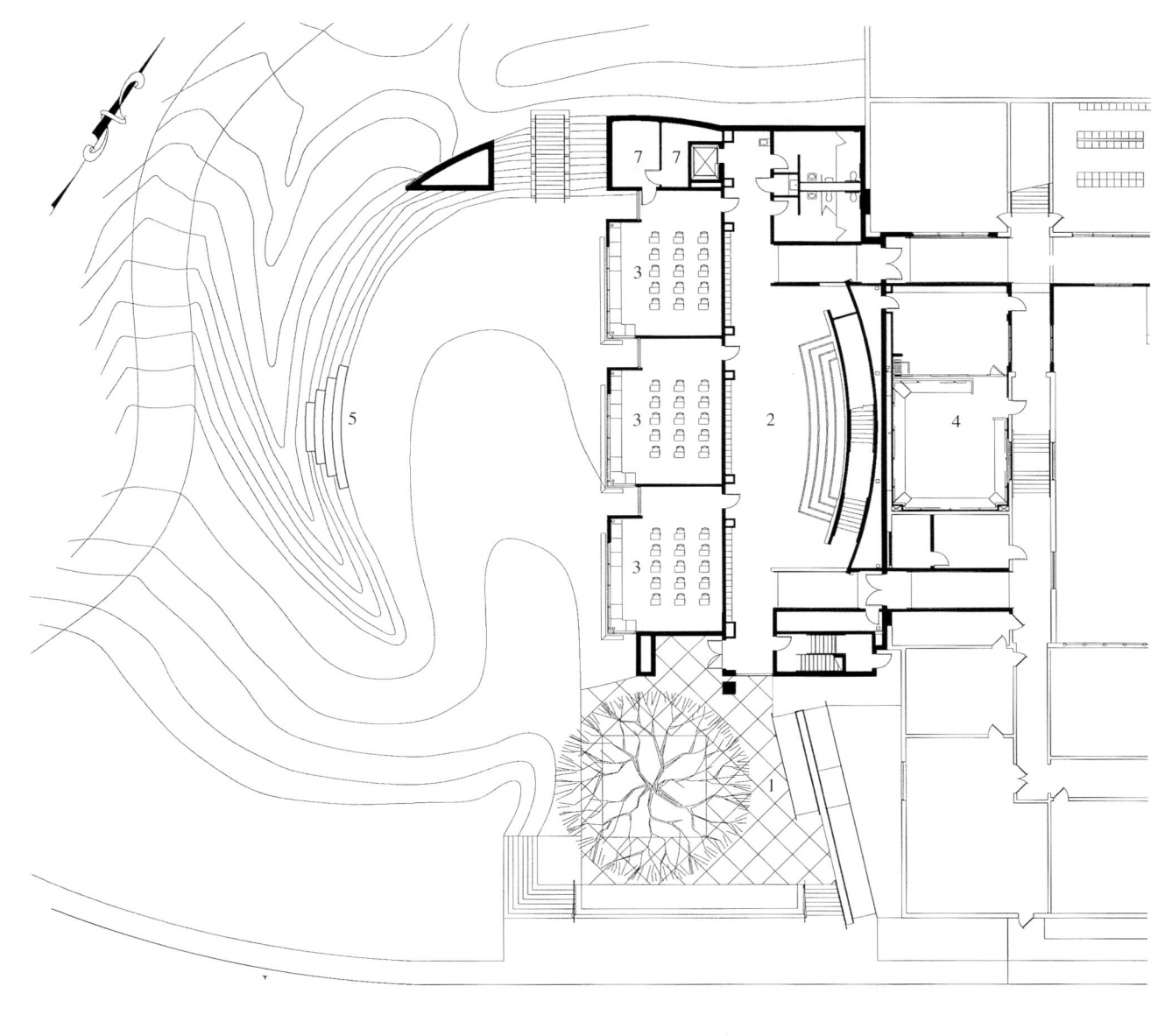

Second floor plan.

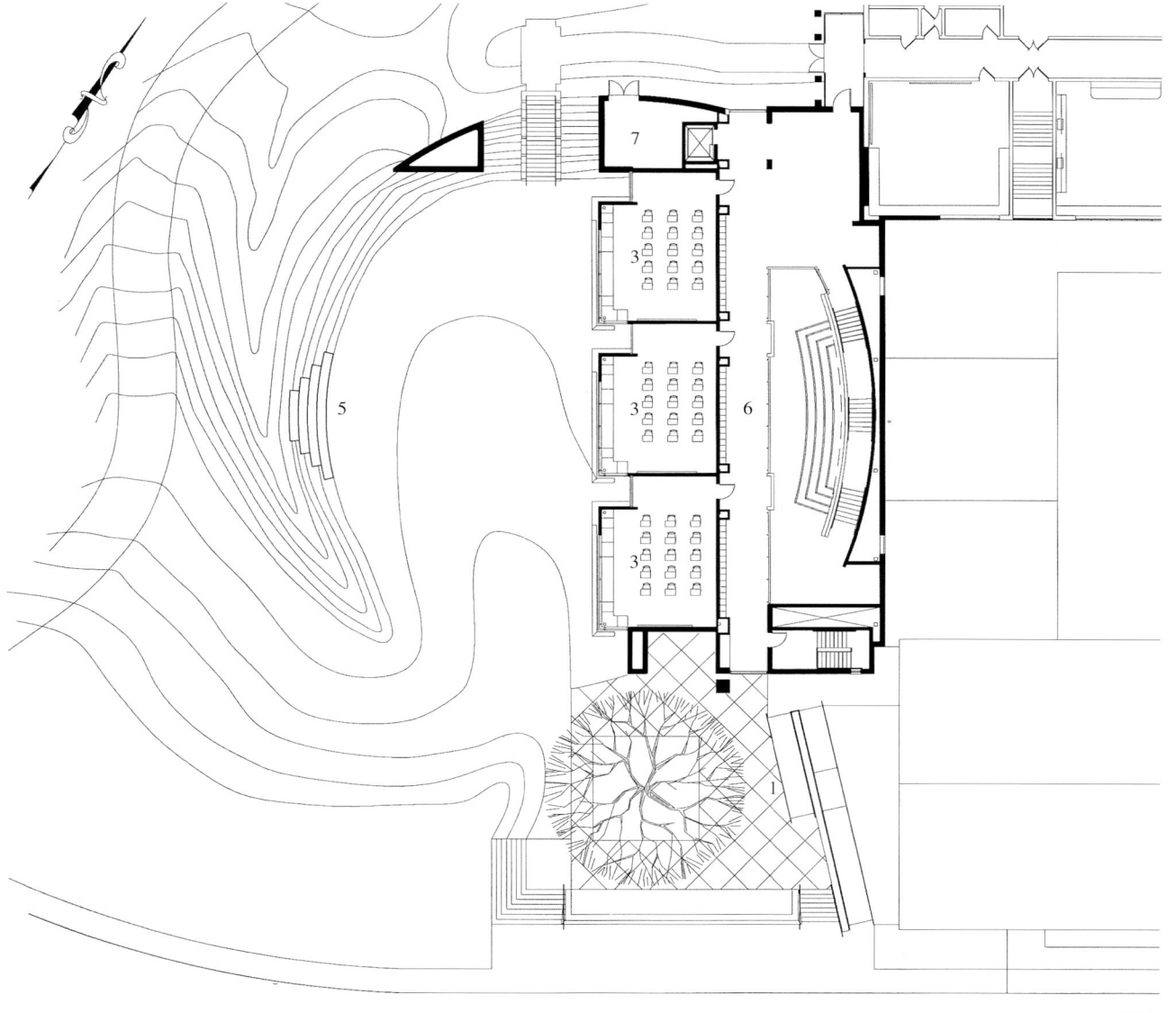

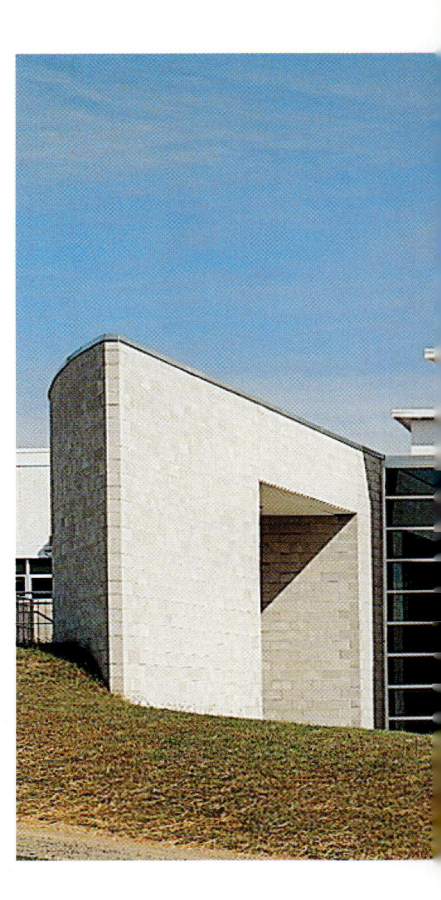

Entry.

Interior amphitheatre.

View of upper level.

West elevation.

View of portal to playing fields.

113

The Village of South Orange is committed to its commercial downtown and views a new arts center as a key element in its revitalization. The new arts center is sited next to the railroad station, which is the centerpiece of a successful streetscape and commercial development plan, and across the street from a proposed new hotel and conference center. South Orange, with its compact historic center, access to commuter transportation and parking, university affiliations, and dynamic leadership, is in a unique position to build an arts center that will act as a magnet and development engine.

The dynamism of film and theatre and the expressiveness of the visual arts provide an impetus for architecture that strongly links interiors to urban spaces. The brick- and stucco-clad volumes are pierced by glass and steel structures that create a high level of transparency for public zones. The life of the building, its lobbies and circulation and banqueting space, is highly visible from the new urban space at the building's entry. A screen-like curved wall serves as a backdrop for people moving up the double-helix stair to the different activities in the building.

The demanding program of a fine-tuned presenting theatre, with accommodation for loading, proper backstage and support activities, as well as all of the special considerations of lighting, acoustics, and access is achieved on two levels within the footprint provided. The arts center will include a 400-seat theatre for music, dance and theatrical productions, a multiplex cinema, a restaurant with gallery space, and a multi-purpose space for use by the Village's Recreation Department. It is designed to complement the strong historic character of the surrounding architecture, and serve as a beacon for pedestrians, riders on the train, and motorists on busy South Orange Avenue.

South Orange, NJ, 2001

South Orange Arts Center

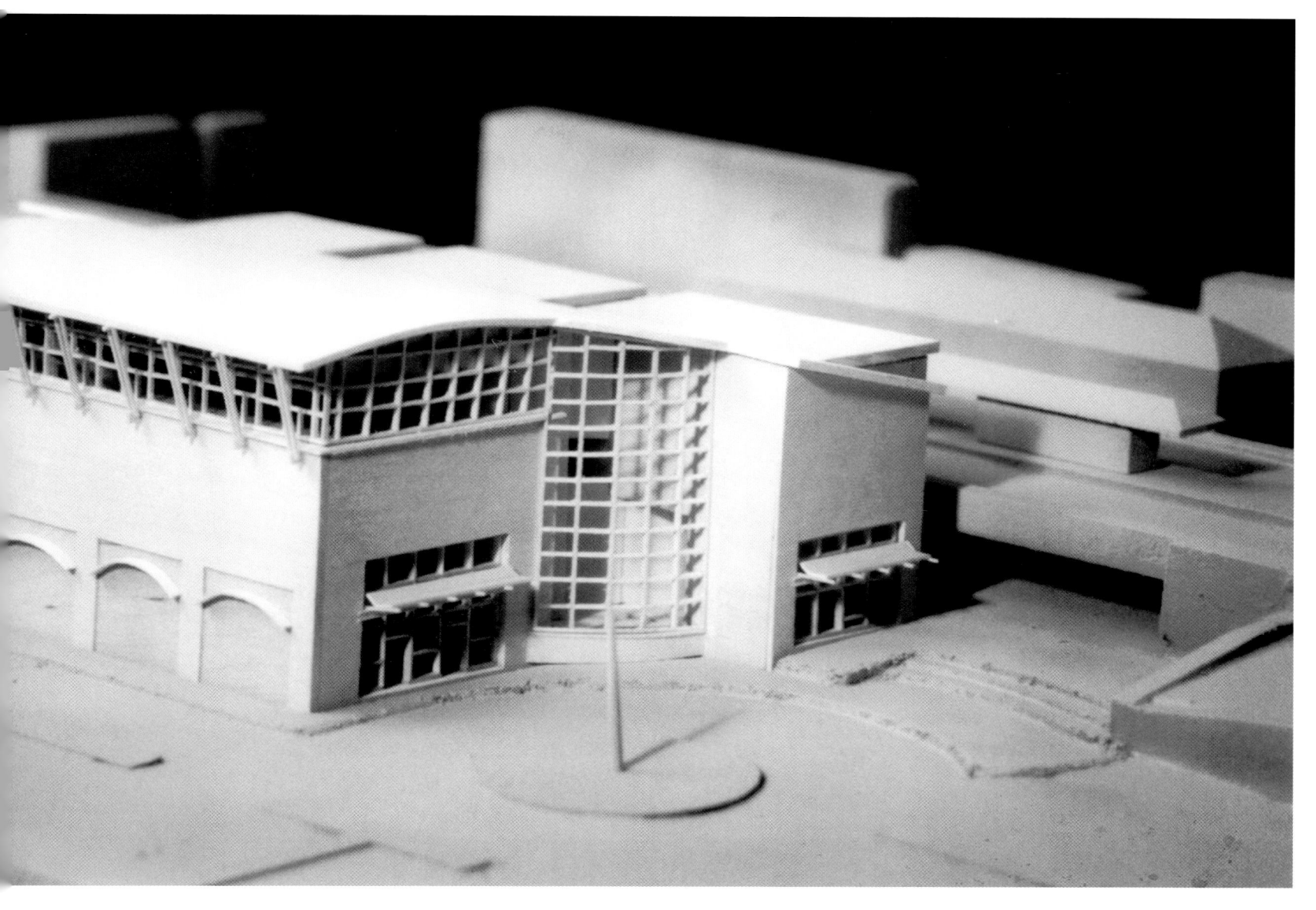

Model, view of entrance.

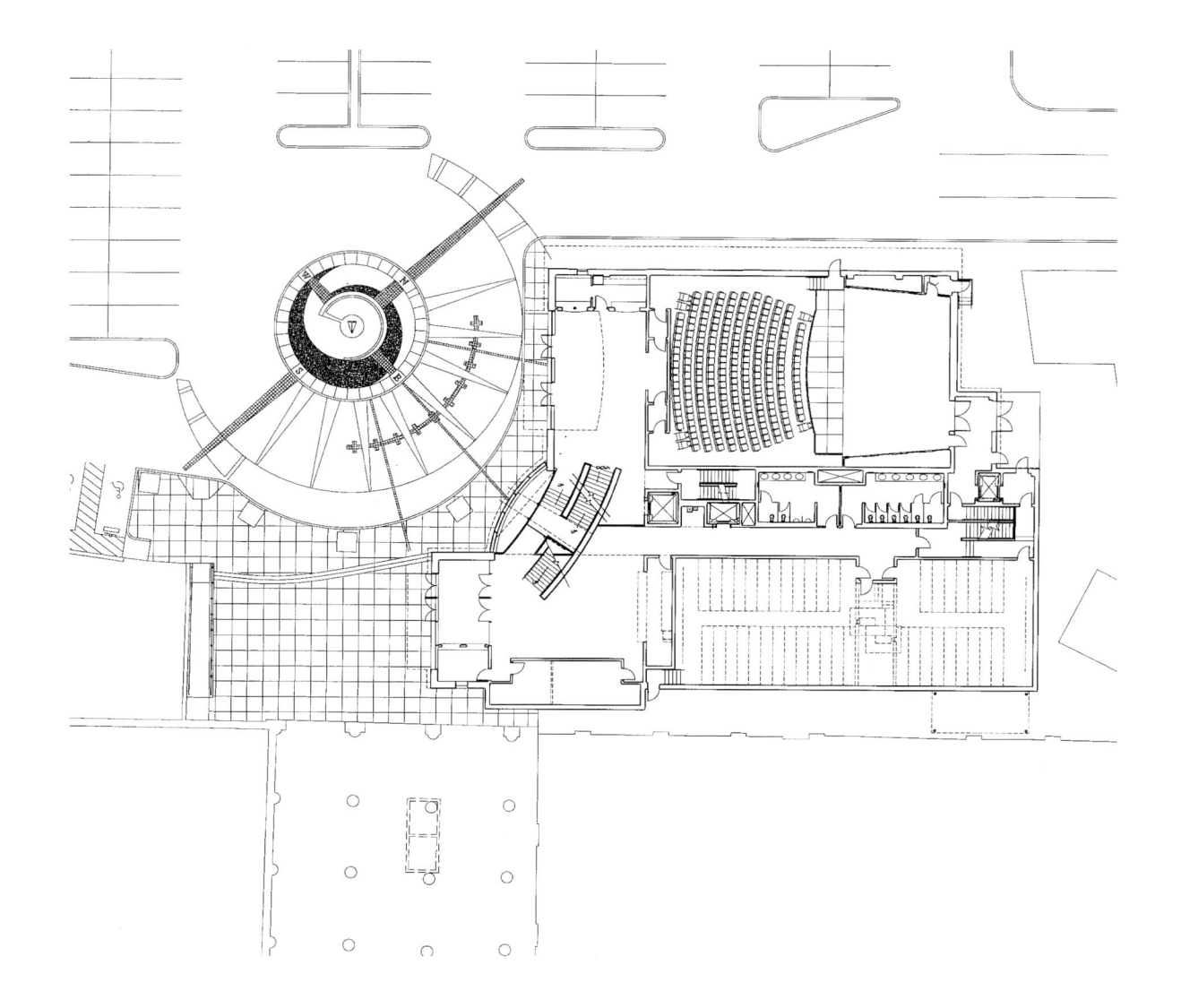

Site plan with first floor.

115

Model night view.

Main stairs.

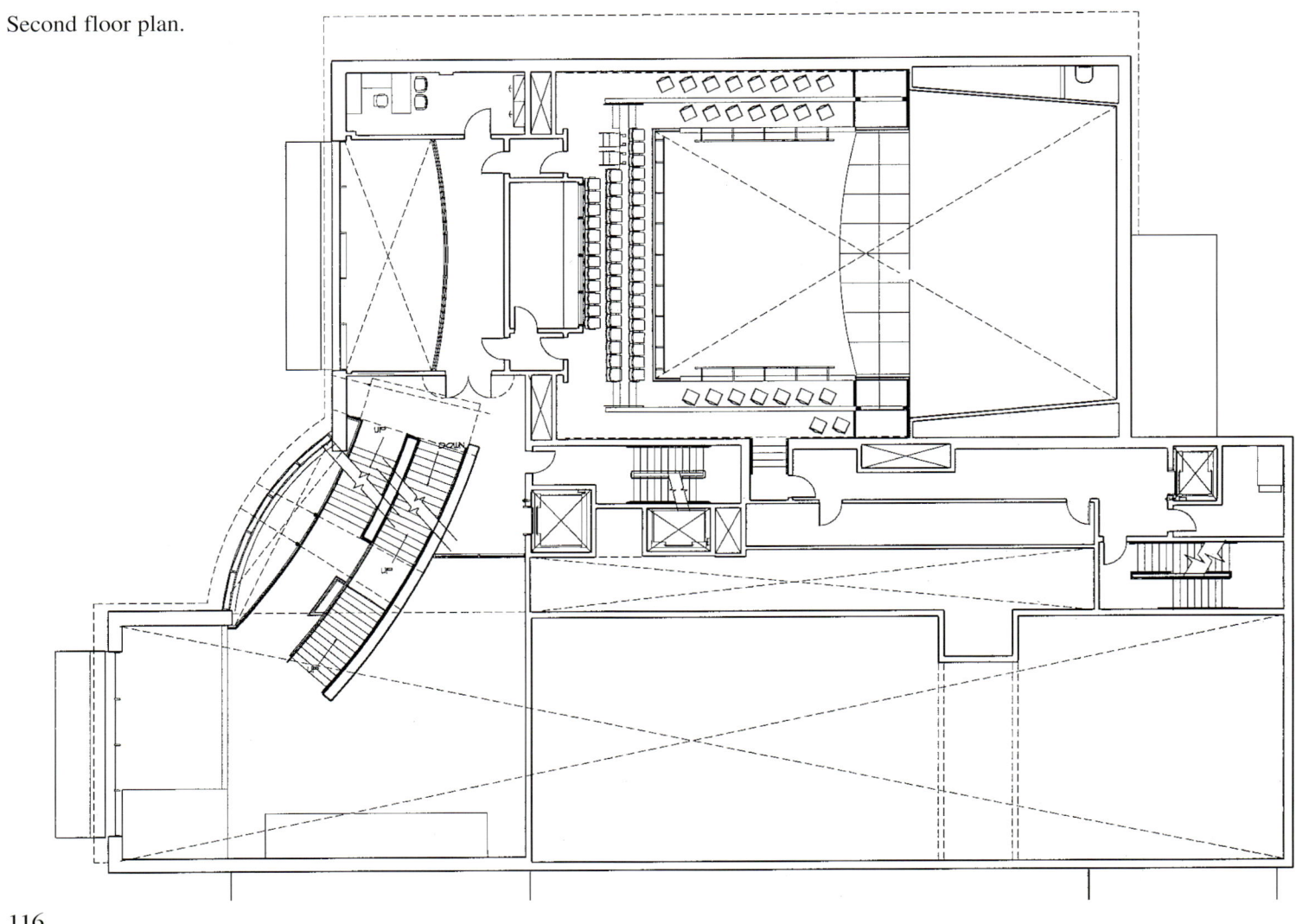

Second floor plan.

Exploded axonometric.

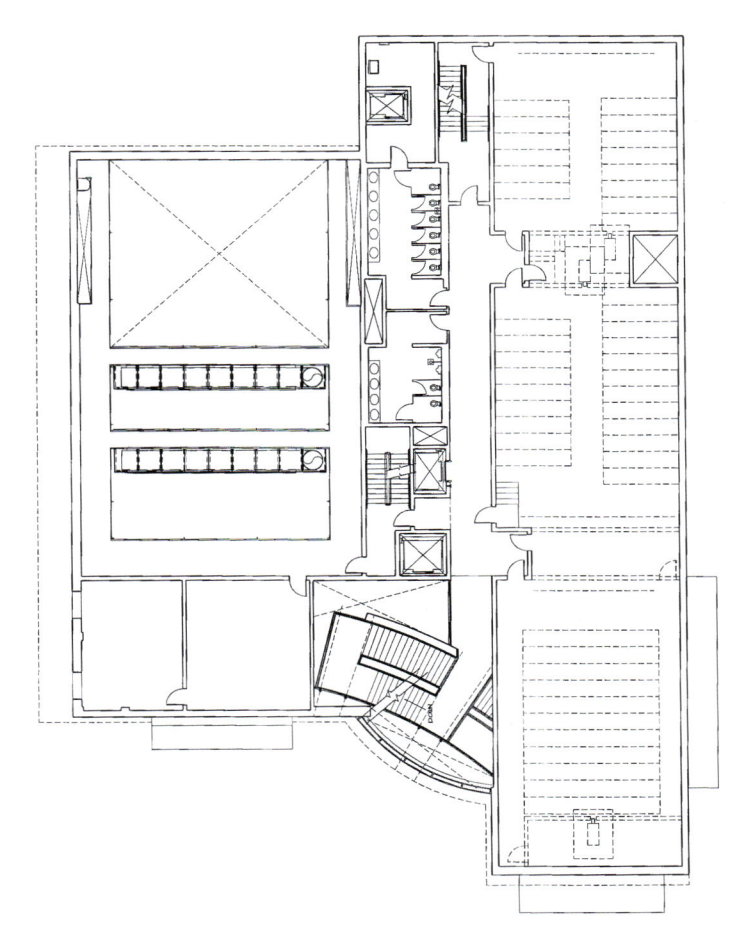

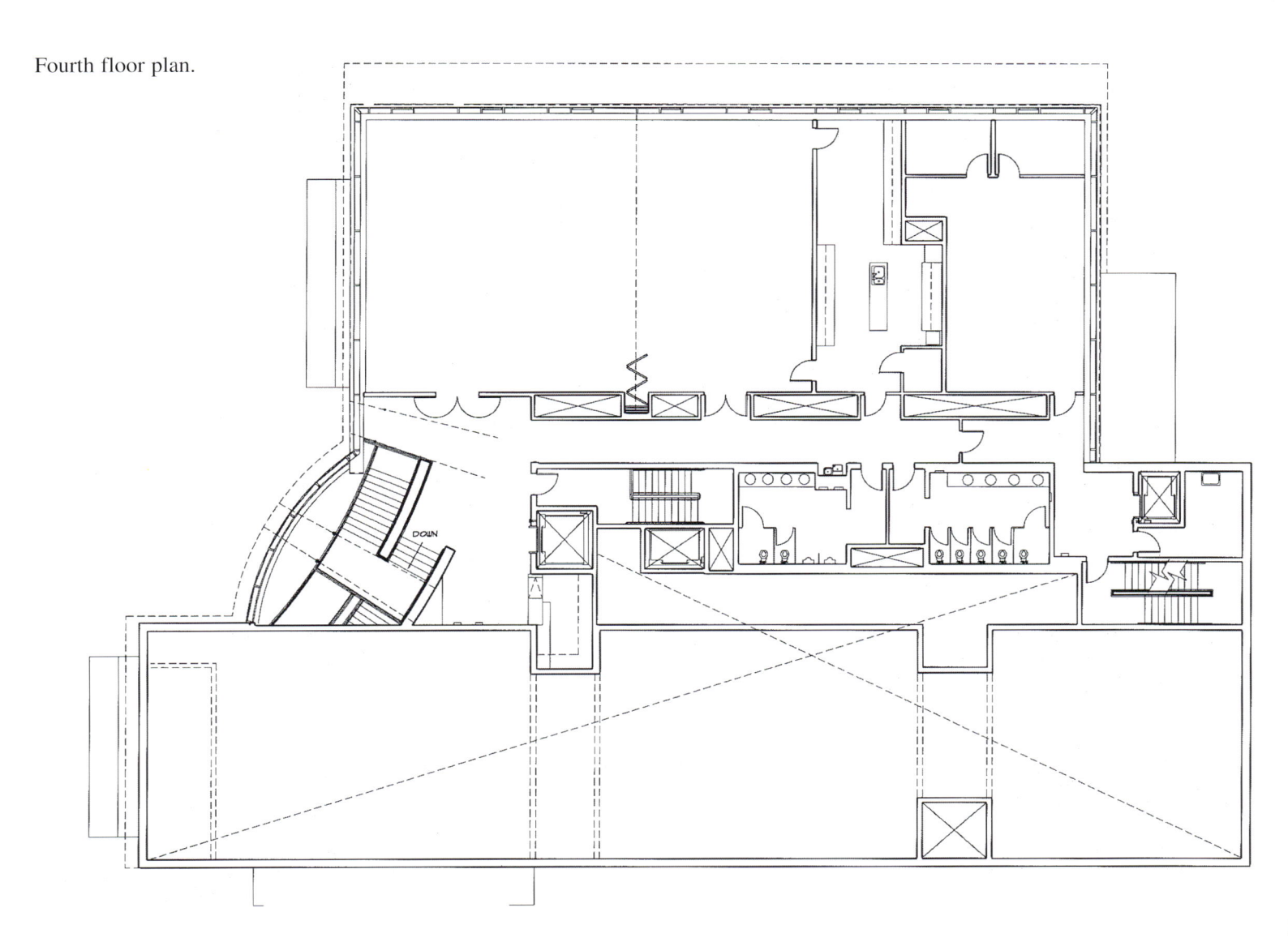

Third floor plan.

Fourth floor plan.

117

Steel Works

This project, the renovation of a 1970s academic building, juxtaposes the art history department's main offices and teaching spaces. Contrasting techtonic systems present a play on the discourse of the discipline. The plan, a double square, is conceived as a pair of slides of two radically different spatial experiences. The lecture room, gallery/lobby, and classroom is an open plan, screened space, with exposed steel structure and articulated assemblies of wood. In sharp contrast, the administrative offices are grouped around a central atrium that appears to be defined by thick walls, load bearing construction with an emphasis on shaped space.

The central entry axis of the composition represents a passage from one spatial order to the other. In a further play on the idea of the projection of images, the lobby/gallery is partially lighted by a suspended fixture that projects an image of the plan on the floor of the space. The entry axis terminates in a traditional icon, a plaster cast of an initiation scene from the Eleusian ceremonies, a not inappropriate expression for the experience of young art historians being initiated into their discipline.

Princeton, NJ, 1997

Department of Art and Archaeology at Princeton University

Lecture room.

Initiation frieze from the Eleusian mysteries.

Gallery/lobby showing ceiling projection.

Plan.	1. Office	5. Entry	9. Work Room
	2. Copy Room	6. Lobby	10. Anteroom
	3. Computer / Mail	7. Auditorium	11. Restroom
	4. Classroom	8. Secretary	12. Reception

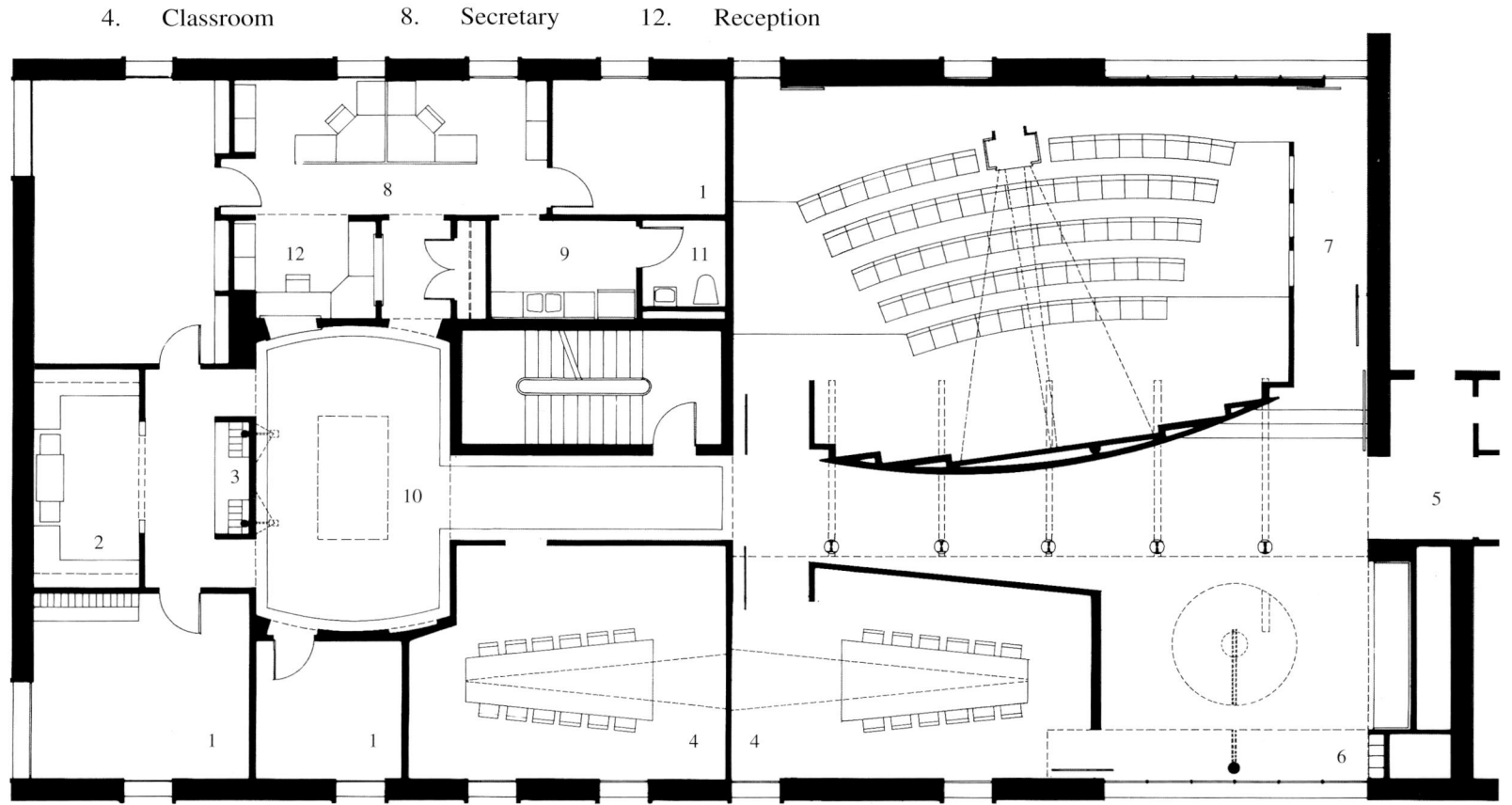

View of main corridor.

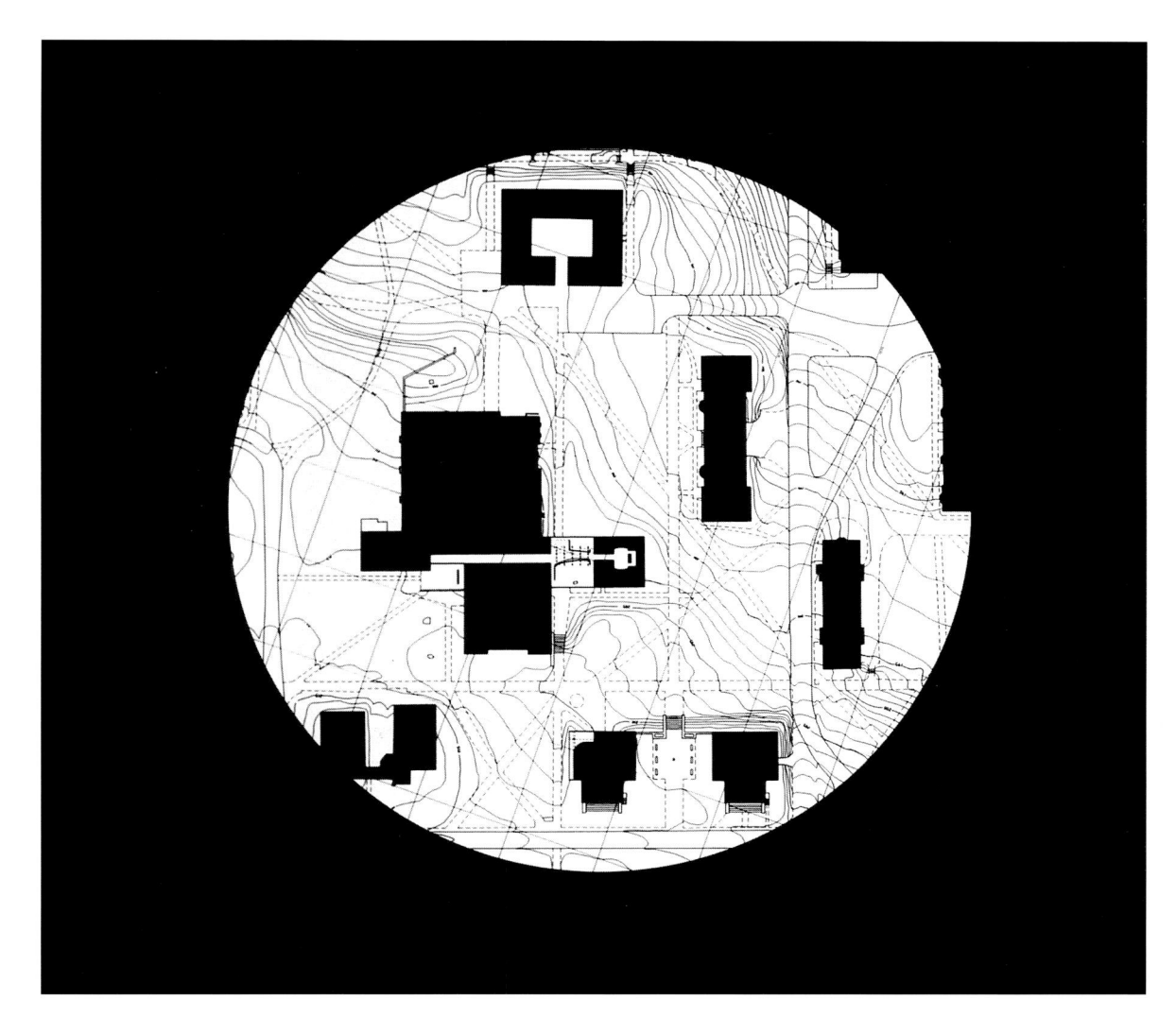

Site plan.

The Cityscape Center Master Plan creates a new vision for ten acres of land at the core of historic New Brunswick. It is proposed that the site, currently dominated by surface parking lots, reflect the unique combination of complementary activities – including university and corporate centers, health care and residential developments, and judicial and entertainment complexes – that have been the source of New Brunswick's resurgence.

The plan's initial organizational gesture is a crossing of two urban axes. One axis will become a major, tree-lined spine of the city, linking the existing hotel/corporate center to the north with new corporate facilities planned for the New Street gateway. The cross axis, starting at the Monument Square theater district, will cross the first and continue to the reconstituted housing, and further to a pedestrian bridge over a highway leading to a riverfront park.

The individual elements of the proposed Cityscape Center plan include a 1250-seat theatre near the existing Monument Square theatre district; a five-screen film complex for the Sundance Festival as part of a larger complex with a café and retail store; 170 market-rate housing units; a riverfront park, connected to the rest of the site by a pedestrian bridge over a highway; a restaurant; an outdoor amphitheatre; 300,000 square feet of corporate offices in new office buildings; a mix of retail; and expanded parking.

Implementation of the Cityscape Center plan will be in phases, with market forces driving the development. The assumption of the plan is that the goals of street making, urban place making, linkage of centers, and cohesive urban fabric can be met with a variety of massing strategies. The emphasis is on creating a pedestrian city that will be animated by the strategic location of complementary uses.

At the completion of this master plan, a new hotel/conference center was added to the program, and is now in schematic design as a major mixed-use anchor of Monument Square. The fifteen-story building will mark the historic heart of the city, and through the master plan linkages to riverfront, corporate centers and university complexes, will strengthen the urban life of this burgeoning city.

New Brunswick, NJ, 1998

Cityscape Center Master Plan

View toward the river.

Axonometric of downtown.

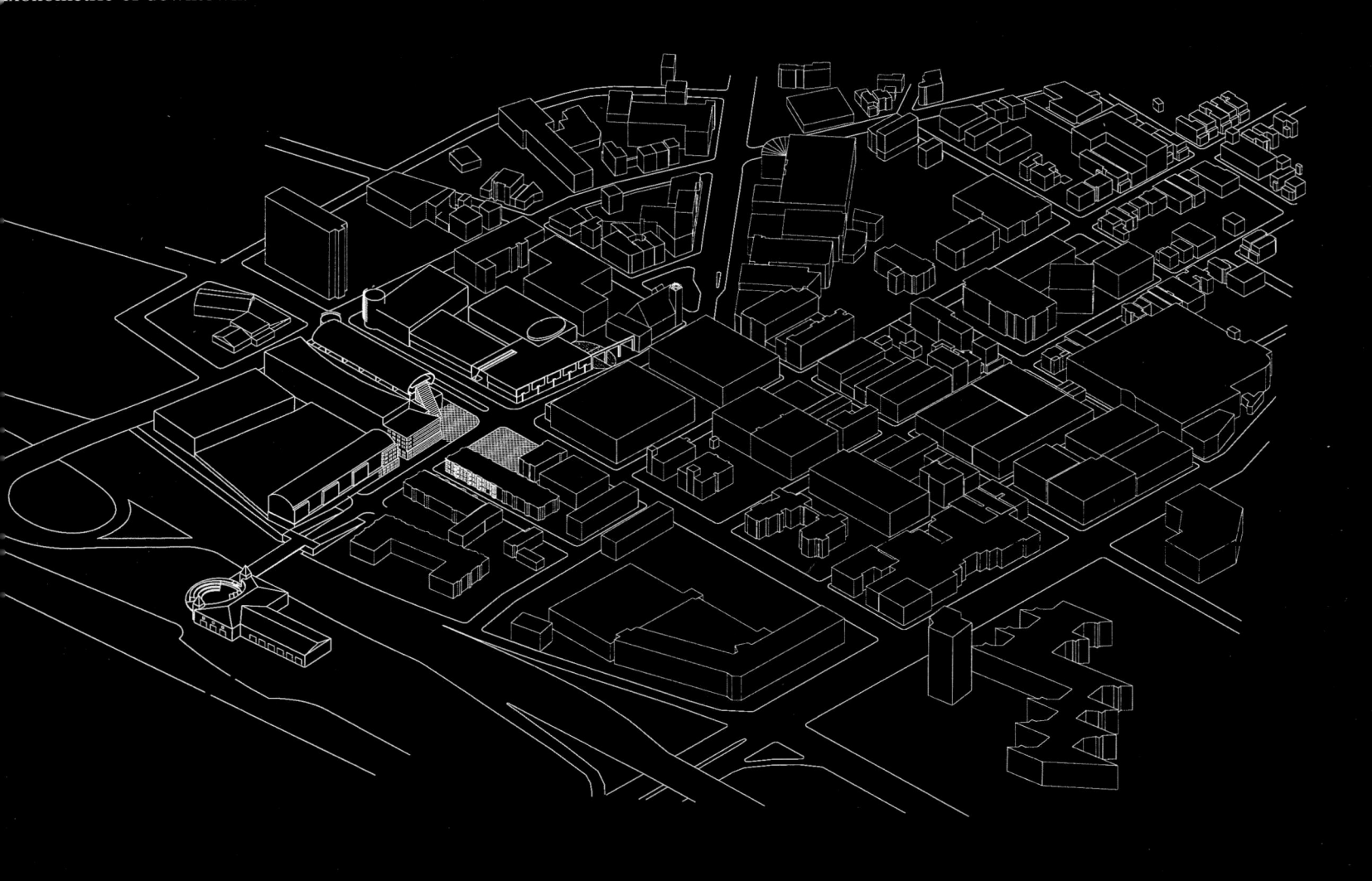

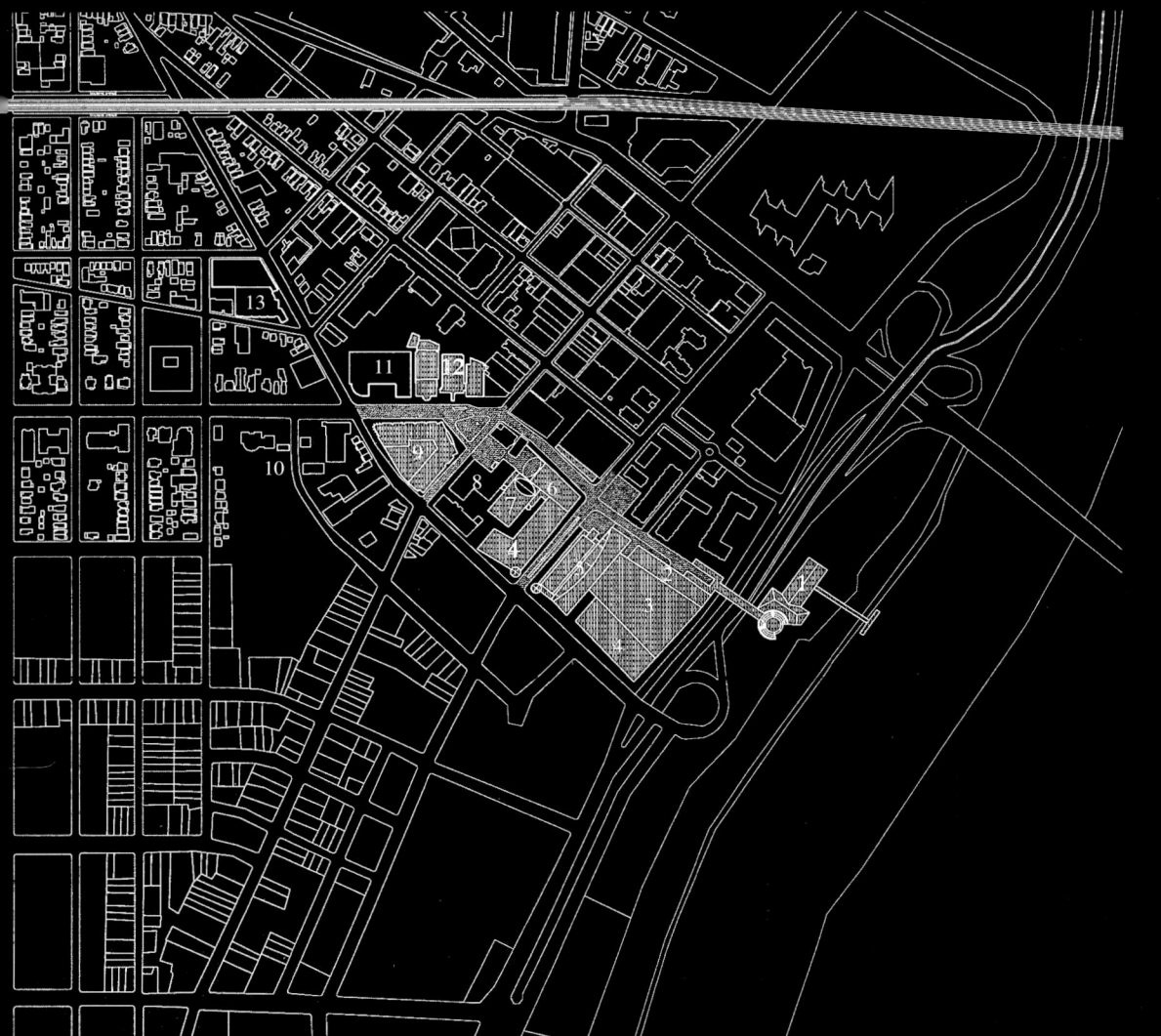

Site Plan

1. Boat House
2. Housing
3. Plaza/Parking below
4. Parking
5. Office
6. Retail
7. Theatre
8. Plaza
9. Heldrich Center and New Brunswick Hotel
10. Henry Guest House
11. Civic Square 1 Building
12. New Brunswick Cultural Center
13. Middlesex County Family Courts Building

Hotel first floor plan.

Hotel second floor plan.

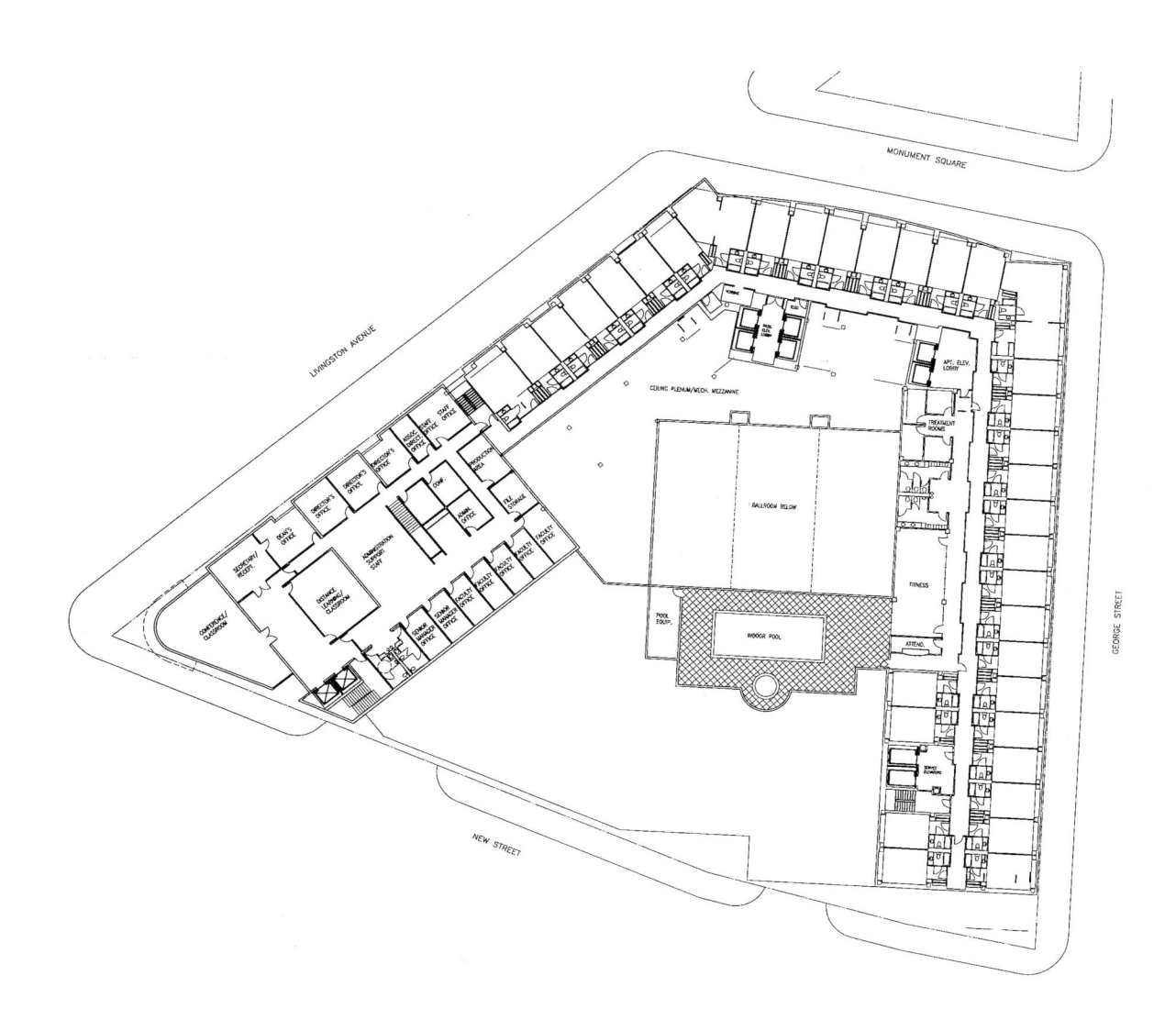

Hotel plans.

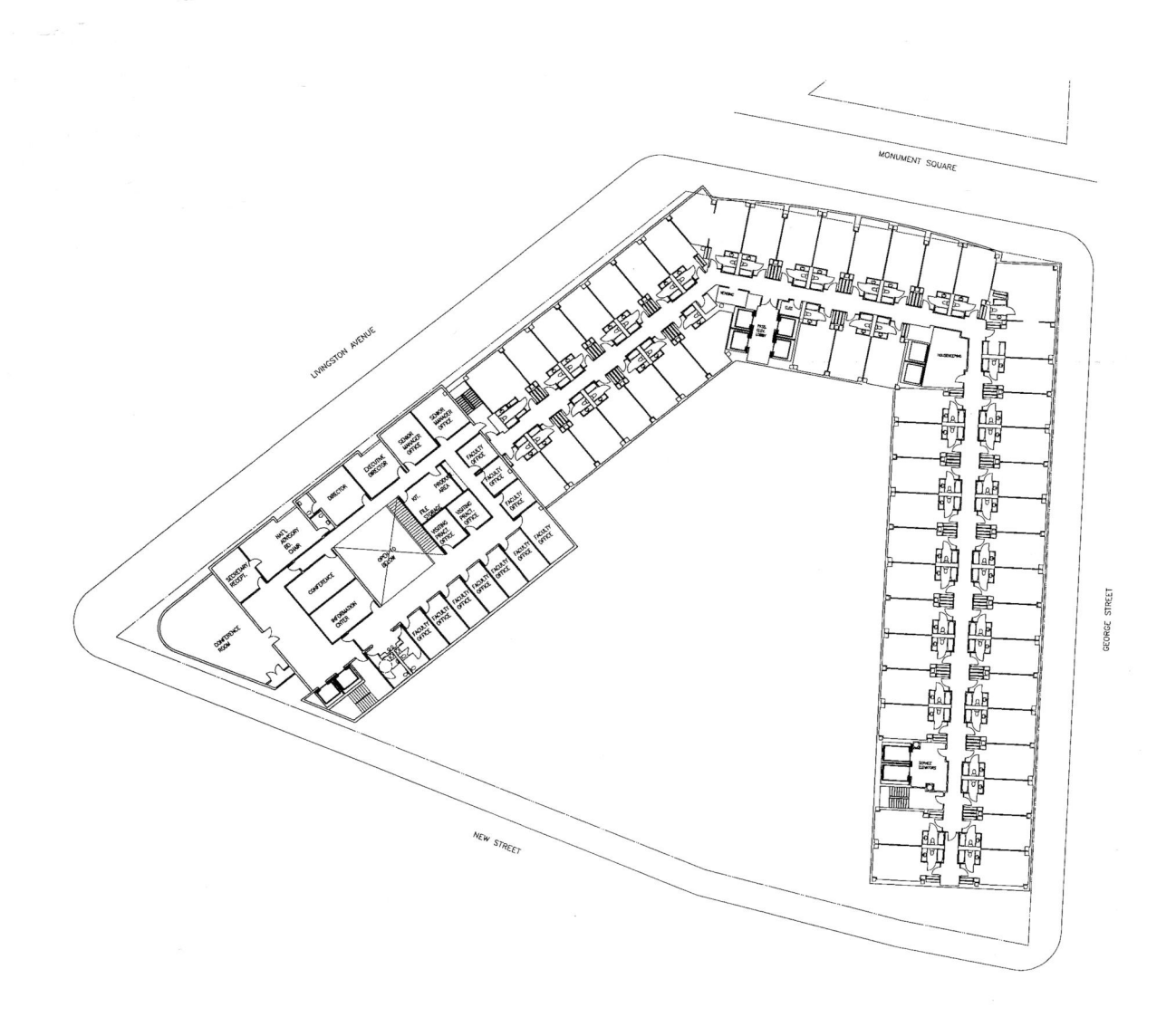

Hotel / Conference Center elevation at Monument Square.

Study model.

This architectural sculpture is the focus of a public park that is the place of arrival in the center of Atlantic City. It serves as beacon and landmark, belvedere and spectacle, folly and sign. Its base is a swirl of landmass and fountains that spiral up to an elevated platform. Views of the city from this room are framed by the piers of the structure, and the view up into the night sky is a vortex formed of steel and teflon fabric. At night, an array of cyber lights are projected onto the structure from points around the site as well as from its lantern. The poem *From the Lighthouse* is inscribed in five tablets that form the floor of the structure.

When you have drained your cup of moon and stars
and waves have knocked your boat and you about,
when sharks have marked your fear and let you fill
your net with weeds and stones or tiny fish
that rush to spill their slippery lives away,

when you have spun your yarn, revised your prayer,
and promised not to leave the ones you left,
when fog obscures the dials and wheels you need,
and salted lashes close down sated eyes,
when you have lost your compass in the sea
(that god who listens closely - where was he?)

and you stand and turn around and around,
you stand and turn the darkness inside out...
when whirling gulls undo the knots you made
and tear your weather-beaten sail like bread.

When your legs collapse and your body, spent,
forgets its dream of reunion with - what?
the lady? mirage, no help, no home, no one
but you unbearably alone and cold,
the certainty of ceaseless drifting...

Sailor be still. I am the pulse of night.
Rely, rely, rely. Not there, but here,
not dark, but light. My perfect eye will burn
away the waves and shine a path for you.
Allow me now to bring you in again

Atlantic City, NJ, 1998   Patricia Farewell

From the Lighthouse

View to the north.

From the Lighthouse 4:00 p.m.

From the Lighthouse 3:00 p.m.

From the Lighthouse 7:00 a.m.

Opposite, from the Lighthouse 10:00 p.m.

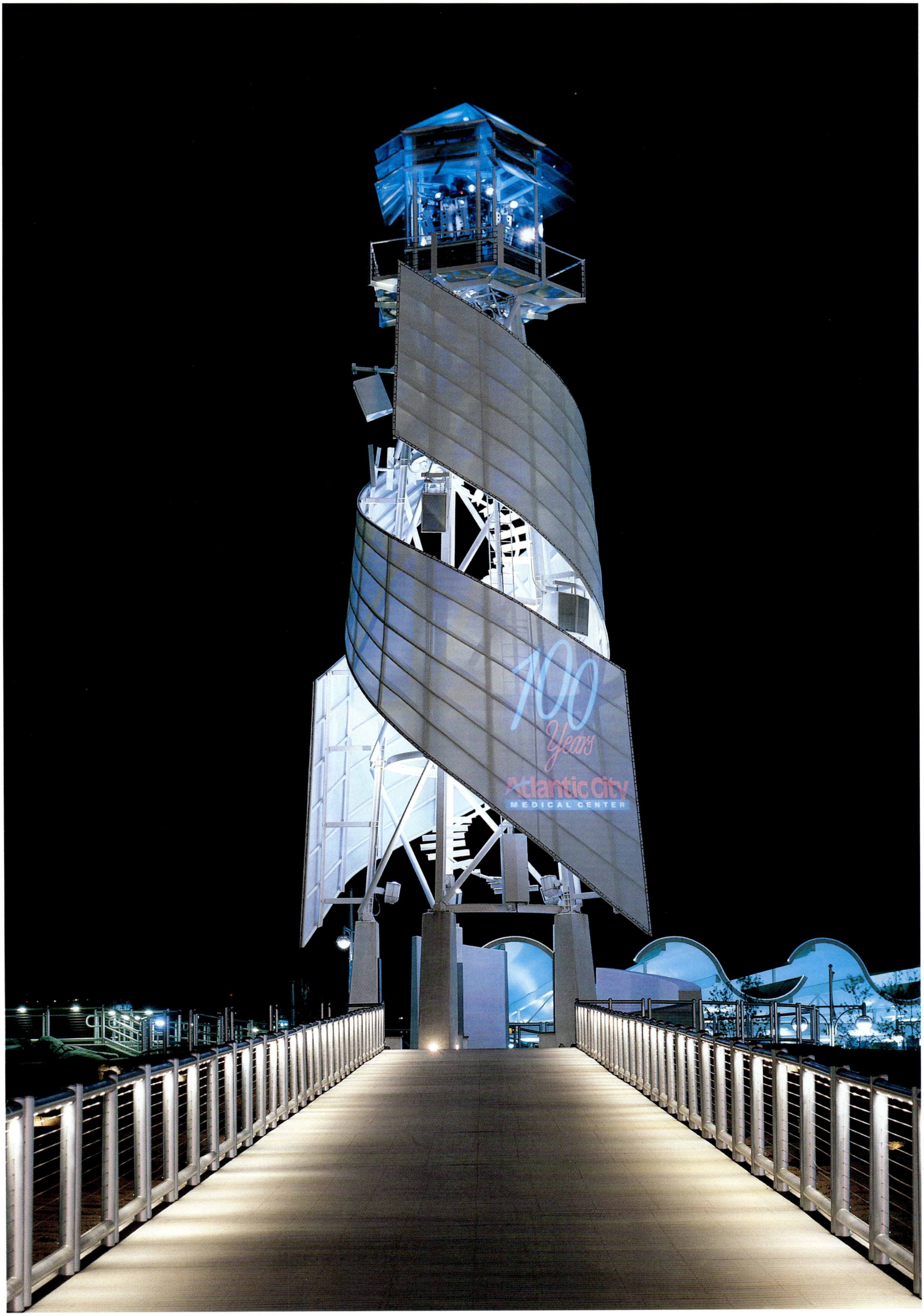
100
Years
Atlantic City
MEDICAL CENTER

Plans 1, 2, 3, 4.

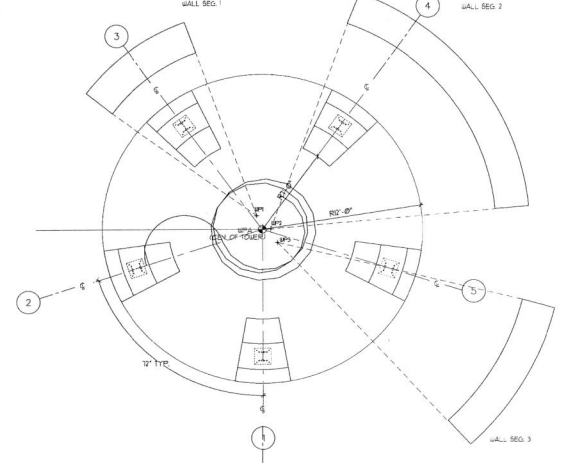

Opposite, view of spiral stair.

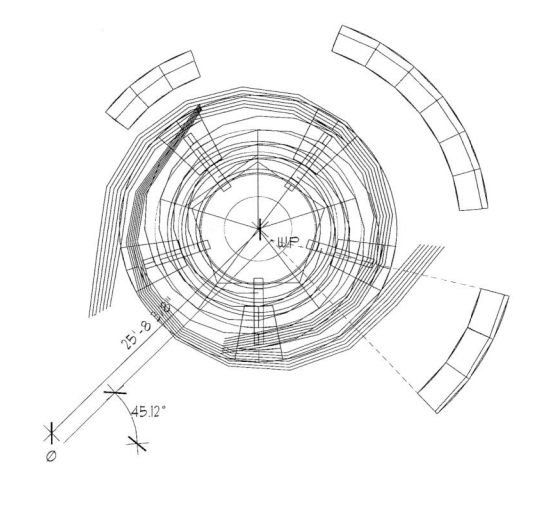

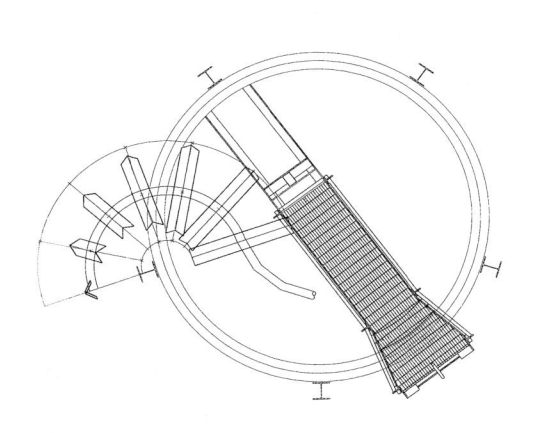

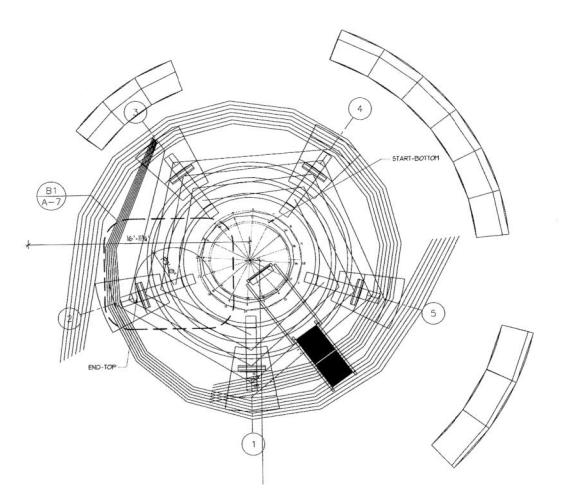

Views to the sky.

134

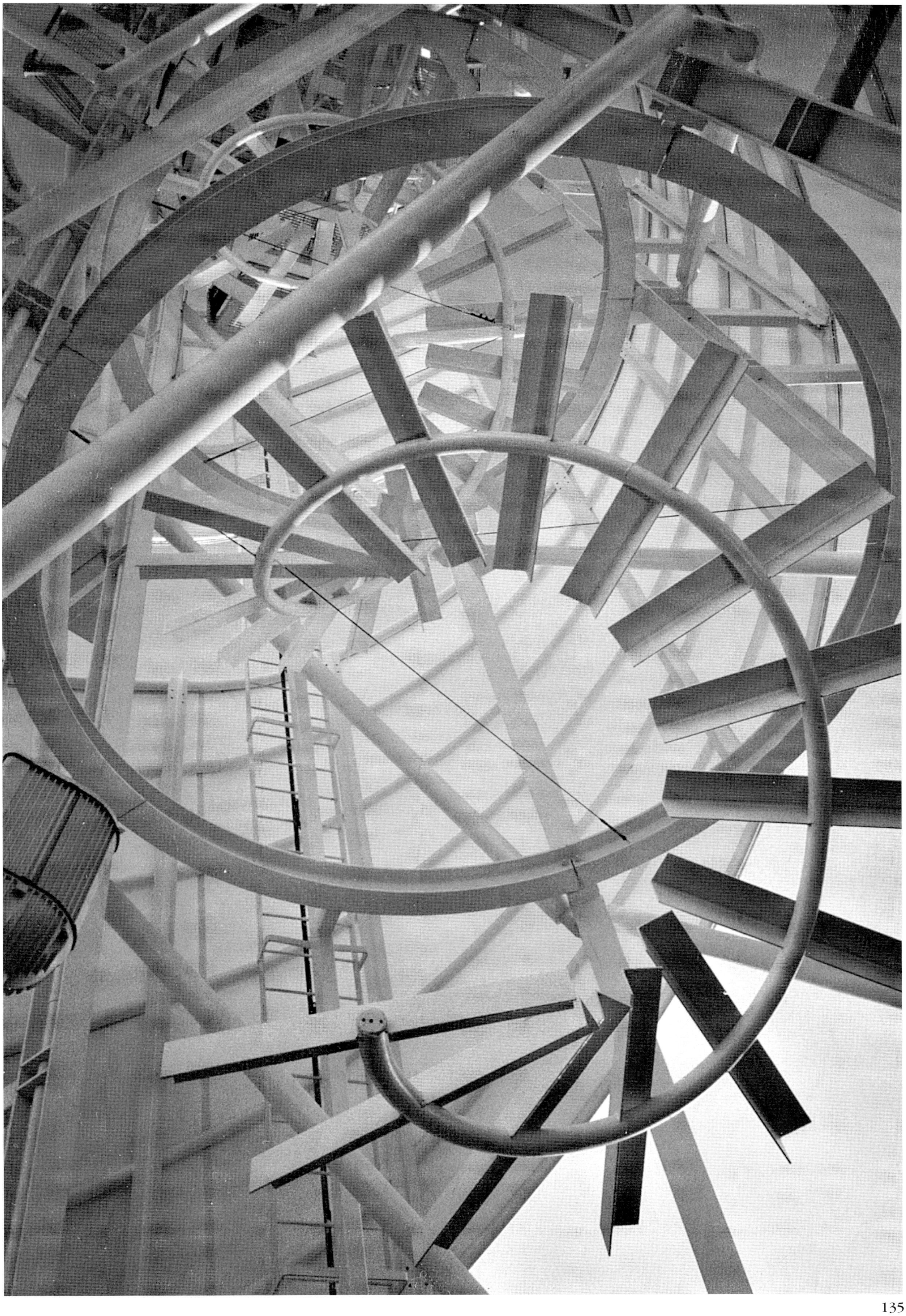

Credits

Crescent Houses at The Lawrenceville School
Project Location: Lawrenceville, NJ
Owner: The Lawrenceville School
No. of Stories: 3
Square Footage: 18,000 each
Project Completion Date: 1987
Publications: Clifford A. Pearson, "School Ways", *Architectural Record*, Vol. 10, 1987; "Design Awards", *Architecture New Jersey*, Issue 4, 1988.
Awards: Excellence in Architecture, 1989, AIA/New Jersey Society of Architects Design Awards Program; New Jersey Historic Sites Council Historic Preservation Awards, 1989, Brick in Architecture Awards Program, Brick Institute of America; Commendation for Proposed Project, 1983, AIA/New Jersey Society of Architects Design Awards Program
Architect of Record: Short and Ford, Architects
Partner in Charge: William H. Short
Designer: Charles Farrell & Michael Farewell
Project Manager: James A. Gatsch
Other FFMG Personnel: James Repka, Mary Horst, Gerry Meagher, David Burton, Marta Anez-Spangler, Alison Baxter
Landscape Design: Philip N. Winslow
Interior Design: Dian Boone
Cost Estimator: Anthony Baionno
Engineers:
Structural: Blackburn Engineering Associates
Mechanical: Kallen and Lemelson
Electrical: Kallen and Lemelson
Plumbing/Fire Protection: Kallen and Lemelson
Civil: Princeton Junction Engineering
Construction Manager: Lehrer McGovern Bovis

Bainbridge House
Project Location: Princeton, NJ
Owner: Historical Society of Princeton
Original Date: ca. 1765
Project Completion Date: ca. 1992
No. of Stories: 2
Square Footage: 5,000
Publications: Access to the Past: How the Americans with Disabilities Act Affects Historic Preservation, Eastern Paralyzed Veterans Association, 1995.
Awards: New Jersey Historic Preservation Commendation, 1994, New Jersey Historic Preservation Office
Architect of Record: Ford Farewell Mills and Gatsch, Architects
Partner in Charge: William H. Short, then Michael J. Mills
Preservation Architect: Michael J. Mills
Project Manager: Alex Lissé
Other FFMG Personnel: Annabelle Radcliffe-Trenner
Lighting Design: Terry, Chassman & Associates
Conservator: Frank Welsh
Engineers:
Structural: Keast & Hood Co.
Mechanical: Seeler-Smith & Associates, Inc.
Electrical: Seeler-Smith & Associates, Inc
Plumbing/Fire Protect: Seeler-Smith & Associates, Inc.
General Contractor: Princeton Construction Group, Inc.

Civic Square I: Center for the Arts and Planning at Rutgers University
Project Location: New Brunswick, NJ
Owner: New Jersey Economic Development Authority
No. of Stories: 5
Project Completion Date: 1995
Square Footage: 160,000
Awards: Excellence in Downtown Development, 1996, Downtown New Jersey, Inc.; Special Recognition, New Jersey Golden Trowel Masonry Awards, 1996, International Masonry Institute
Architect of Record: Ford Farewell Mills and Gatsch, Architects
Associated Architect: Cope Linder Associates
Partner in Charge: James A. Gatsch
Designer: Michael Farewell
Project Manager: David E. McWilliams
Other FFMG Personnel: William A. Gittings, Alison Baxter, Kelly DeLong, Nicholas Cusano
Landscape Design: Cope Linder Associates
Interior Design: Ford Farewell Mills and Gatsch, Architects
Lighting Design: Lighting Design Collaborative
Acoustical Consultant: Shen Milsom & Wilke
Engineers:
Structural: Cagley & Harman
Mechanical: Syska & Hennessy, Inc.
Electrical: Syska & Hennessy, Inc.
Plumbing/Fire Protection: Syska & Hennessy, Inc.
Civil: French and Parello, Associates, PA
Other Consultants: Parking: Walker Parking
Geo-Tech: French and Parello, Associates, PA
Construction Manager: Keating Building Corporation

New Jersey Historical Society
Project Location: Newark, NJ
Owner: New Jersey Historical Society
Original Architect: Guilbert & Betelle
Original Date: 1926
No. of Stories: 5
Square Footage: 35,000
Project Completion Date: 1997
Awards: New Jersey Historic Preservation Award, 1998, New Jersey Historic Preservation Office; Excellence in Downtown Development, 1999, Downtown New Jersey, Inc.; Donald J. Dust Award, 1998, Newark Landmarks and Historic Preservation Committee
Architect of Record: Ford Farewell Mills and Gatsch, Architects
Partner in Charge: Michael J. Mills
Preservation Architect: Michael J. Mills
Project Manager: Anne E. Weber
Other FFMG Personnel: Douglas R. Wasama, Michael Tartaglia, Alison Baxter, Kelly DeLong, Ira Guterman, Richard Olszewski, Chris Boyer, Karen R. Sargent
Conservator: George Wheeler
Cost Estimator: Anthony Baionno
Engineers:
Structural: Robert Silman Associates
Mechanical: Ford Farewell Mills and Gatsch, Architects
Electrical: Ford Farewell Mills and Gatsch, Architects
Plumbing/Fire Protection: AMM Technical
Civil: Frank Lehr Associates
General Contractor: York Hunter

F.M. Kirby Shakespeare Theatre for the New Jersey Shakespeare Festival at Drew University
Project Location: Madison, NJ
Owner: New Jersey Shakespeare Festival
Original Date: 1909
Project Completion Date: 1998
No. of Stories: 3
Square Footage: 18,000
Publications: "Shakespeare on Campus", *Entertainment Design*, March 1999; Sara Nuss-Galles, "To Build, Perchance to Rebuild", *Drew*, Summer 1998
Awards: Award for Merit, USITT Architecture Awards Program, 1999, United States Institute for Theatre Technology, Inc.; Best of Education-Advanced, New Jersey Golden Trowel Masonry Awards, 1998, International Masonry Institute;
Best Restored Project, BAC Craft Award, 1998, International Union of Bricklayers & Allied Craftworkers
Architect of Record: Ford Farewell Mills and Gatsch, Architects
Partner in Charge: Michael Farewell
Designer: Michael Farewell
Project Manager: Michael Schnoering
Other FFMG Personnel: Laurence Capo, Andrew Guzik, Chris Boyer, Kelly DeLong, Ira Guterman, Richard Olszewski
Landscape Design: Bohler Engineering Associates, PC
Interior Design: Ford Farewell Mills and Gatsch, Architects
Lighting Design: Ford Farewell Mills and Gatsch, Architects
Theater Consultant: Fisher/Dachs Associates
Acoustical Consultant: Jaffe Holden Scarbrough Acoustics, Inc.
Conservator: Integrated Conservation Resources
Cost Estimator: Turner Construction Company
Engineers:
Structural: Harrison-Hamnett, PC
Mechanical: Ford Farewell Mills and Gatsch, Architects
Electrical: Ford Farewell Mills and Gatsch, Architects
Plumbing/Fire Protection: AMM Technical
General Contractor: Damon G. Douglas Company

Legislative Chambers and Administrative Areas of the New Jersey State House
Project Location: Trenton, NJ
Owner:State of New Jersey
Original Architect: Jonathan Doane & others
Original Date: 1793
No. of Stories: 4
Square Footage: 150,000
Project Completion Date: 1991
Publications: Susan Doubilet, "New Jersey State House Restoration", *Building Renovation*, Nov-Dec 1992; "Design Awards", *Architecture New Jersey*, Issue I, 1993
Awards : New Jersey Historic Preservation Award, 1996, New Jersey Historic Preservation Office; Excellence in Architecture, 1992, AIA/New Jersey Society of Architects Design Awards Program
Architect of Record: Joint Venture Architects - Short and Ford/Johnson Jones
Partner in Charge: Jeremiah Ford III
Managing Partner: George Jones
General Manager: James A. Gatsch
Design Architect: Michael Farewell
Preservation Architect: Michael J. Mills
Programming Architect: Walter Maykowskyj

Production Architect: Harry Labold
Other JVA Personnel: Matthew Chalifoux, Joseph Alperstein, Anne E. Weber, Mary Wasserman, Alison Baxter, Chuck Johnson, Gonzolo Rizo-Patron, John Hatch, Oliver Franklin, Moses King-Nabi, Earl McQueen, Jr., and many others
Interior Design: Hughes Group Ltd.
Acoustical Consultant: KMK Associates
Conservator: Building Conservation Associates
Cost Estimator: MMP or Lehrer McGovern Bovis
Engineers:
Structural: Blackburn Engineering
Mechanical: J.R. Loring and Associates
Electrical: J.R. Loring and Associates
Plumbing/Fire Protection: J.R. Loring and Associates
Civil: VEP
Other Consultants: Paint Analysis: Frank S. Welsh; *Paint Analysis:* Biltmore Campbell Smith; *Scagliola:* Ahmed Sulieman; *Stained Glass:* McKernan Satterless Associates; *Archaeology:* Hunter Research
Construction Manager: Lehrer McGovern Bovis

South Addition to the New Jersey State House
Project Location: Trenton, NJ
Owner: State of New Jersey
No. of Stories: 2
Square Footage: 37,500
Project Completion Date: 1991
Publications: Susan Doubilet, "New Jersey State House Restoration", *Building Renovation*, Nov-Dec 1992;
"Design Awards", *Architecture New Jersey*, Issue I, 1993
Awards: NJ Historic Preservation Award, 1996, NJHPO; Excellence in Downtown Development, 1993, Downtown NJ, Inc.; Excellence in Architecture, 1992, AIA/New Jersey Society of Architects Design Awards Program; 1st Place-Renovation/Restoration, 1991, New Jersey State Conference of Bricklayers and Allied Craft
Architect of Record: Joint Venture Architects - Short and Ford/Johnson Jones
Partner in Charge: Jeremiah Ford III
Managing Partner: George Jones
General Manager: James A. Gatsch
Design Architect: Michael Farewell
Preservation Architect: Michael J. Mills
Programming Architect: Walter Maykowskyj
Production Architect: Harry Labold
Other JVA Personnel: Joseph Alperstein, Mary Wasserman; Alison Baxter, Chuck Johnson, Gonzolo Rizo-Patron, John Hatch, Oliver Franklin, Moses King-Nabi, Earl McQueen, Jr., Elizabeth Cooke, Mary Horst, and many others
Landscape Design: Miceli Kulik Williams and Associates
Interior Design: Joint Venture Architects
Lighting Design: Lighting Design Collaborative
Cost Estimator: MMP or Lehrer McGovern Bovis
Engineers:
Structural: Blackburn Engineering
Mechanical: J.R. Loring and Associates
Plumbing/Fire Protection: J.R. Loring and Associates
Civil: Edwards & Kelcey
Construction Manager: Lehrer McGovern Bovis

Pool, Pool House and Landscape II
Project Location: Fisher's Island, NY

Owner: Judith-Ann Corrente
No. of Stories: 1
Project Completion Date: 1993
Publications: Thomas Fisher, "Two Poolhouses, One Client", *Progressive Architecture*, June 1993
Julie V. Iovine, "A Dip Into Antiquity", *The New York Times Magazine*, June 20, 1993 Leanne Boepple, "Stone Passages Enclose Homeowner's Poolside Niche", *Stone World*, April 1994; "Design Awards", *Architecture New Jersey*, Issue I, 1993
Awards: Design Award for Excellence, 1993, New York Council, Society of American Registered Architects; Excellence in Architecture, 1992, AIA/New Jersey Society of Architects Design Awards Program; Gold Award, 1992, NJEPA
Architect of Record: Ford Farewell Mills and Gatsch, Architects
Partner in Charge: Michael Farewell
Designer: Michael Farewell
Project Manager: Gonzalo Rizo-Patron
Other FFMG Personnel: Joseph Gallagher, Suzanne McGeorge
Landscape Design: Ford Farewell Mills and Gatsch, Architects
Interior Design: Ford Farewell Mills and Gatsch, Architects & Kline Stewart
Lighting Design: Ford Farewell Mills and Gatsch, Architects
Engineers:
Structural: Harrison-Hamnett, PC
General Contractor: William Swale, Jr.

Princeton University Graduate College
Project Location: Princeton, NJ
Owner: Princeton University
Original Architect: Ralph Adams Cram
Original Date: 1912 & 1928
No. of Stories: 3 to 4
Square Footage: 150,000
Project Completion Date: 1993
Awards: Award of Merit, 1994, AIA/New Jersey Society of Architects Design Awards Program; Recognition for Interior Rehabilitation, 1993, Historical Society of Princeton
Architect of Record: Ford Farewell Mills and Gatsch, Architects
Partner in Charge: Michael J. Mills
Preservation Architect: Michael J. Mills
Project Manager: Mark Kirby
Other FFMG Personnel: Alison Baxter, Alex Lissé, Carl Burns, Jeffrey A. Fleisher, Julie Yang, Christina Sym, Linda Strange, Jennifer Stark, Mary Wasserman
Acoustical Consultant: Acentech
Conservator: Building Conservation Associates
Engineers:
Structural: French and Parello, Associates, PA
Mechanical: Seeler-Smith & Associates, Inc.
Electrical: Seeler-Smith & Associates, Inc.
Plumbing/Fire Protection: Seeler-Smith & Associates, Inc.
Other Consultants: Specifications: Robert Schwartz
Construction Manager: Lehrer McGovern Bovis

Somerset County Courthouse
Project Location: Somerville, NJ
Owner: County of Somerset
Original Architect: James Reily Gordon
Original Date: 1909
No. of Stories: 3

Square Footage: 30,000
Project Completion Date: 1996
Awards: Gold Award for Excellence in Architecture, 1998, AIA/New Jersey Society of Architects Design Awards Program; Best of Restoration, New Jersey Golden Trowel Awards, 1997, International Masonry Institute; Excellence in Downtown Development, 1997, Downtown New Jersey, Inc.
Architect of Record: Ford Farewell Mills and Gatsch, Architects
Partner in Charge: Michael J. Mills
Preservation Architect: Michael J. Mills
Project Manager: Joanna M. Kendig, then Matthew S. Chalifoux
Other FFMG Personnel: Michael Tartaglia, Michael Schnoering, Karen R. Sargent, Mary Wasserman, Douglas R. Wasama, Alex Lissé, Anne E. Weber
Lighting Design: J.R. Loring and Associates
Acoustical Consultant: Acentech
Conservator: Building Conservation Associates
Cost Estimator: Anthony Baionno
Engineers:
Structural: French and Parello, Associates
Mechanical: J.R. Loring and Associates
Electrical: J.R. Loring and Associates
Plumbing/Fire Protection: J.R. Loring and Associates
Other Consultants: Paint Analysis: Frank Welsh; Stained Glass: McKernam Satterlee Associates
General Contractor: Hall Construction Company

Civic Square III: Middlesex County Courthouse
Project Location: New Brunswick, NJ
Owner 1: New Brunswick Development Corporation
Owner 2: Keating Development Corporation
No. of Stories: 4
Square Footage: 98,000
Project Completion Date: 2000
Awards: Grand Award, New Jersey Golden Trowel Masonry Awards, 2000, International Masonry Institute; Best of Municipal/Community, New Jersey Golden Trowel Masonry Awards, 2000, International Masonry Institute
Architect of Record: Ford Farewell Mills and Gatsch, Architects
Partner in Charge: James A. Gatsch
Designer: Michael Farewell
Project Manager: Alison Baxter
Other FFMG Personnel: Mark Vicente, Andrew Guzik, Martha d'Avila, Jennifer Sparrow, Mary Wilson
Landscape Design: Ford Farewell Mills and Gatsch, Architects
Interior Design: Ford Farewell Mills and Gatsch, Architects
Lighting Design: Lighting Design Collaborative
Acoustical Consultant: Shen Milsom & Wilke
Engineers:
Structural: Cagley Harman & Associates
Mechanical: Giovanetti Shulman Associates
Electrical: Giovanetti Shulman Associates
Plumbing/Fire Protection: Giovanetti Shulman Associates
Civil: Birdsall Engineering
Construction Manager: Keating Building Corporation

Princeton Child Development Institute
Project Location: Lawrence Township, NJ
Owner: Princeton Child Development Institute
No. of Stories: 1

Square Footage: 20,000
Project Completion Date: 1996
Awards: Silver Award for Excellence in Architecture, 1997, AIA/New Jersey Society of Architects Design Awards Program
Architect of Record: Ford Farewell Mills and Gatsch, Architects
Partner in Charge: Michael Farewell
Designer: Michael Farewell
Project Manager: Michael R. Schnoering
Other FFMG Personnel: Nicholas P. Cusano, Alison Baxter, Jeffrey A. Fleisher, Ira Guterman, Richard Olszewski
Landscape Design: Van Cleef Engineering Associates
Interior Design: Ford Farewell Mills and Gatsch, Architects
Lighting Design: Ford Farewell Mills and Gatsch, Architects
Cost Estimator: Anthony Baionno
Engineers:
Structural: Harrison-Hamnett, PC
Mechanical: Ford Farewell Mills and Gatsch, Architects
Electrical: Ford Farewell Mills and Gatsch, Architects
Plumbing/Fire Protection: AMM Technical
Civil: Van Cleef Engineering Associates
General Contractor: E. Allen Reeves, Inc.

New Jersey Housing & Mortgage Finance Agency
Project Location: Trenton, NJ
Owner: New Jersey Housing & Mortgage Finance Agency
Original Date: circa 1928
No. of Stories: 1
Square Footage: 67,000
Project Completion Date: 1995
Publications: M.J. Madigan, "New Jersey Housing and Mortgage Finance Agency", *Interiors,* March 1997
Awards: Citation of Merit, 1996, AIA/New Jersey Society of Architects Design Awards Program; Excellence in Downtown Development, 1996, Downtown New Jersey, Inc.; Special Recognition, 1996, NJ Golden Trowel Masonry Awards, International Masonry Institute; Business Week/Architectural Record Award, 1999
Architect of Record: Joint Venture Architects - Ford Farewell Mills and Gatsch/Johnson Jones
Partner in Charge: James A. Gatsch
Designer: Michael Farewell
Project Manager: Harry LaBold
Other JVA Personnel: Nicholas P. Cusano, George Jones, Cathy Counts, Kevin S. Dunn, Camille Bailey, Ira Guterman
Interior Design: Joint Venture Architects
Lighting Design: Lighting Design Collaborative
Cost Estimator: T.R.I. Berman
Engineers:
Structural: French and Parello, Associates
Mechanical: Ford Farewell Mills and Gatsch, Architects
Electrical: J.R. Loring and Associates
Plumbing/Fire Protection: J.R. Loring and Associates
Construction Manager: T.R.I. Berman

University Cottage Club Library
Project Location: Princeton, NJ
Owner: University Cottage Club
No. of Stories: 3
Project Completion Date: 1992
Awards: Historical Society of Princeton, 1993, Recognition for Implementing a Comprehensive preservation Plan

Architect of Record: Ford Farewell Mills and Gatsch, Architects
Partner in Charge: Jeremiah Ford III
Preservation Architect: Michael J. Mills
Project Manager: Alex Lissé
Other FFMG Personnel: Ann Leopold
Conservator: Building Conservation Associates, Inc.
Cost Estimator: Ford Farewell Mills and Gatsch, Architects
Engineers:
Electrical: Seeler-Smith & Associates, Inc.
General Contractor: Mark Reed Restorations

Pool and Pool House I
Project Location: Far Hills, NJ
Owner: Judith-Ann Corrente
No. of Stories: 1
Project Completion Date: 1991
Publications: Thomas Fisher, "Two Poolhouse, One Client", *Progressive Architecture,* June 1993; Tracie Rozhon, "The Pool House: Making a Stylish Splash", *The New York Times,* July 2, 1995
Awards: Designs of the Year, 1992, Residential Architecture, *New Jersey Monthly*
Architect of Record: Ford Farewell Mills and Gatsch, Architects
Partner in Charge: Michael Farewell
Designer: Michael Farewell
Project Manager: Michael R. Schnoering
Other FFMG Personnel: Dean Donatelli, Victor Sittig
Landscape Design: Ford Farewell Mills and Gatsch, Architects
Interior Design: Ford Farewell Mills and Gatsch, Architects
Lighting Design: Ford Farewell Mills and Gatsch, Architects
Cost Estimator: Anthony Baionno
Engineers:
Structural: Harrison-Hamnett, PC
Mechanical: Ford Farewell Mills and Gatsch, Architects
Electrical: Ford Farewell Mills and Gatsch, Architects
Plumbing/Fire Protection: Ford Farewell Mills and Gatsch, Architects
Civil: Apgar Engineering
General Contractor: Inca Pools

Casino Building at Georgian Court College
Project Location: Lakewood, NJ
Owner: Georgian Court College
Original Architect: Bruce Price
Original Date: 1890's
Project Completion Date: 1996
No. of Stories: 2
Square Footage: 60,000
Architect of Record: Ford Farewell Mills and Gatsch, Architects
Partner in Charge: Michael J. Mills
Designer: Michael Farewell
Preservation Architect: Anne E. Weber
Project Manager: Anne E. Weber
Other FFMG Personnel: Karen R. Sargent, William G. Gittings, Ira Guterman, Richard Olszewski
Conservator: Integrated Conservation Resources
Cost Estimator: Anthony Baionno
Engineers:
Structural: Harrison-Hamnett, PC
Mechanical: Ford Farewell Mills and Gatsch, Architects
Electrical: Ford Farewell Mills and Gatsch, Architects
Plumbing/Fire Protection: AMM Technical

Civil: Hopewell Valley Engineering
Other Consultants: Roofing: H.B. Fishman & Company
General Contractor: E. Allen Reeves, Inc.

Far Hills Country Day School
Project Location: Far Hills, NJ
Owner: Far Hills Country Day School
No. of Stories: 2
Square Footage: 12,000
Project Completion Date: 1997
Awards: Gold Award for Excellence in Architecture, 1998, AIA/New Jersey Society of Architects Design Awards Program
Architect of Record: Ford Farewell Mills and Gatsch, Architects
Partner in Charge: Michael Farewell
Designer: Michael Farewell
Project Manager: Michael Schnoering, then Chris Boyer
Other FFMG Personnel: Alison Baxter, Nicholas P. Cusano, Kelly DeLong, Ira Guterman, Richard Olszewski
Landscape Design: Ford Farewell Mills and Gatsch, Architects
Interior Design: Ford Farewell Mills and Gatsch, Architects
Lighting Design: Ford Farewell Mills and Gatsch, Architects
Cost Estimator: Anthony Baionno
Engineers:
Structural: Harrison-Hamnett, PC
Mechanical: Ford Farewell Mills and Gatsch, Architects
Electrical: Ford Farewell Mills and Gatsch, Architects
Plumbing/Fire Protection: AMM Technical
General Contractor: E. Allen Reeves, Inc.

South Orange Arts Center
Project Location: South Orange, NJ
Owner: Township of South Orange Village
No. of Stories: 3
Square Footage: 36,000
Project Completion Date: 2001
Architect of Record: Ford Farewell Mills and Gatsch, Architects
Partner in Charge: Michael Farewell
Designer: Michael Farewell
Project Manager: Michael Schnoering
Other FFMG Personnel: Quinn Schwenker; Ira Guterman, Richard Olszewski
Landscape Design: Ford Farewell Mills and Gatsch, Architects
Interior Design: Ford Farewell Mills and Gatsch, Architects
Lighting Design: Lighting Design Collaborative
Theater Consultant: Fisher/Dachs Associates
Acoustical Consultant: Jaffe Holden Scarbrough Acoustics, Inc.
Cost Estimator: Anthony Baionno
Engineers:
Structural: Schoor DePalma
Mechanical: Ford Farewell Mills and Gatsch, Architects
Electrical: Ford Farewell Mills and Gatsch, Architects
Plumbing/Fire Protect: AMM Technical
Civil: Schoor DePalma

Department of Art and Archaeology at Princeton University
Project Location: Princeton, NJ
Owner: Princeton University
Project Completion Date: 1993
Square Footage: 10,400
Publications: Detailing Light: Integrated Lighting Solutions for Residential and Contract Design, by Jean Gorman, Watson-Guptill Publications, 1995; *Architecture New Jersey,* issue 4:1992
Architect of Record: Ford Farewell Mills and Gatsch, Architects
Partner in Charge: Michael Farewell
Designer: Michael Farewell
Project Manager: Gonzalo Rizo-Patron
Interior Design: Ford Farewell Mills and Gatsch, Architects
Lighting Design: Ford Farewell Mills and Gatsch, Architects
Engineers:
Structural: Harrison-Hamnett, PC
Mechanical: Syska & Hennessy, Inc.
Electrical: Syska & Hennessy, Inc.
Plumbing/Fire Protect: Syska & Hennessy, Inc.
General Contractor: Durell Builders

Cityscape Center Master Plan
Project Location: New Brunswick, NJ
Owner: New Brunswick Development Corporation
Project Completion Date: 1998
Square Footage: 10 Acres
Architect of Record: Ford Farewell Mills and Gatsch, Architects
Partner in Charge: Michael Farewell
Designer: Michael Farewell
Project Manager: Alison Baxter
Other FFMG Personnel: Elizabeth Holah, Martha d'Avila
Engineers:
Civil: Birdsall Engineering

From the Lighthouse
Project Location: Atlantic City, NJ
Owner: Casino Reinvestment Development Authority
Project Completion Date: 1998
Publications: Julie V. Iovine, "Yes if by Land (No if by Sea): Lighting the Way to Atlantic City", *The New York Times,* January 8, 1998; "An Inland Lighthouse Serves as an Urban Marker", *Architectural Record,* January 1999; Louis M. Brill, Beacon in the Night, *Signs of the Times,* March 1999
Awards: Merit Award, 1999, New Jersey Chapter of the American Society of Landscape Architects; Bronze Award for Excellence in Architecture, 1997, AIA/New Jersey Society of Architects Design Awards Program; American Architecture Award, 2000, The Chicago Athenaeum: Museum of Architecture and Design
Architect of Record: Ford Farewell Mills and Gatsch, Architects
Partner in Charge: Michael Farewell
Designer: Michael Farewell
Project Manager: Nicholas P. Cusano, then Michael R. Schnoering
Other FFMG Personnel: Nicholas P. Cusano, Tse-Chiang Leng, Harry Pell, Ira Guterman, Richard Olszewski
Landscape Design: Miceli Kulik Williams and Associates
Lighting Design: Stone Mountain Lasers, Inc.
Engineers:
Structural: Harrison-Hamnett, PC
Mechanical: Ford Farewell Mills and Gatsch, Architects
Electrical: REB Designs
Construction Manager: York Hunter
General Contractor: L. Feriozzi Concrete Co.; Dover Plat & Tank

Firm History

Ford Farewell Mills and Gatsch, Architects grew out of a firm founded in 1974 by William Short (formerly of Venturi and Short) and Jeremiah Ford, III (formerly of Walker Sander Ford and Kerr). Short and Ford was a community-based general practice that undertook both historic preservation and new design projects, primarily residential and small-scale commercial and institutional work.   In 1983, Charles Farrell was added to the partnership, and in 1986, Michael Farewell, Michael Mills, and James Gatsch became partners. With William Short's death in 1991, and Charles Farrell's departure two years later, the firm became known as Ford Farewell Mills and Gatsch.

The work of the last decade and a half, represented by the projects documented in this volume, reveals the firm's continuing emphasis on building within the local community and the broader mid-Atlantic region. The focus of the work is institutional and educational buildings, an outgrowth of earlier work in both new design and historic preservation. The firm's projects have frequently involved major cultural and civic institutions, including the New Jersey State House Complex, Princeton University, and the New Jersey Historical Society.

The dual nature of the firm has become its distinguishing characteristic and reflects a collaborative effort. Michael Farewell is lead designer, while Michael J. Mills directs preservation work. James A. Gatsch is the firm's managing partner, and firm founder Jeremiah Ford continues to focus on community service and special projects.

The most provocative projects are frequently new buildings and additions that engage the historic and the contemporary. As documented in this volume, the attention to material and the craft of building underlies both the new design and historic preservation work. But perhaps the most identifiable feature of this diverse body of work is its emphasis on architecture that engages the occupant in a theatrical experience. This is an architecture which, through memory and sensory delight, intensifies and makes dramatic the act of habitation.

List of Employees

Michael Farewell, FAIA	Partner
Charles A. Farrell, AIA	Partner
Jeremiah Ford III, AIA	Partner
James A. Gatsch, AIA	Partner
Michael J. Mills, FAIA	Partner
William Short, FAIA	Partner
Alison L. Baxter, AIA	Senior Associate
Ira H. Guterman, P.E.	Senior Associate
Joanna M. Kendig, AIA	Senior Associate
Mark W. Kirby, AIA	Senior Associate
David E. McWilliams, AIA	Senior Associate
Lorine Murray-Mechini, AIA	Senior Associate
Michael R. Schnoering, AIA	Senior Associate
Douglas R. Wasama, AIA	Senior Associate
Anne E. Weber, AIA	Senior Associate
Joseph W. Alperstein, AIA	Associate
Nancy Balmer-Csira, AIA	Associate
Chris O. Boyer, AIA	Associate
Marc Brahaney, AIA	Associate
Paul P. Buda, AIA	Associate
Carl K. Burns, AIA	Associate
Laurence Capo	Associate
Matthew S. Chalifoux, AIA	Associate
Nicholas P. Cusano, AIA	Associate
George A. Fett, AIA	Associate
Heidi L. Fichtenbaum, AIA	Associate
William G. Gittings, AIA	Associate
Alison Harris	Associate
Christopher E. Holm, AIA	Associate
Keith Hone, AIA	Associate
Alexander Lisse', AIA	Associate
Gerard R. Meagher, AIA	Associate
Richard S. Olszewski	Associate
Annabelle Radcliffe-Trenner, AIA	Associate
Gonzalo Rizo-Patron, AIA	Associate
Robert N. Rossi, AIA	Associate
Karen R. Sargent, AIA	Associate
Mark B. Vicente, AIA	Associate
Mary Wasserman	Associate

Kenneth R. Abrams
Alissa D. Agnello
Susan Agnello
Robert J. Allen
Ryan S. Amend
Erik M. Anhorn
Nilo M. Apolstol
Susan H. Barbaree
Casey P. Barish
Maria-Isabel Beas
Karen Beloff
Joan E. Berkey
Arthur R. Bifulco
Robert J. Blakeman
Carrie A. Bocci
Dawn Z. Bocian
Rhonda D. Borlaza
Betty A. Bowers
Frederick K. Bowman
Jessica J. Bozarth
Alexander F. Brent
Susan H. Britton
David T. Brown
Merritt Bucholz
William J. Bula
Sarah E. Burchfield
Lisa A. Burke
David J. Burton
Meredith Arms Bzdak
Karen Callaway

Cynthia J. Cameron
Elisabeth Cappelleri
Katryna Carter
Jean A. Cevasco
Susan M. Cevasco
Joshua Chaiken
Anthony T. Chianese
Charles H. Chichester
Yun Shang Chiou
Jae-Hak Chung
Laura H. Citron
Barbara H. Conlon
Elizabeth W. Cooke, AIA
Karis T. Cornell
Paul A. Damiano, AIA
Celeste D. Daniels
Kurt J. Dannwolf
Martha C. M. d'Avila
William R. Davis
Gerald J. DeBlois
Kelly A. DeLong
Neal R. Deputy
Patricia L. DeVito
Karen A. Dewan
Peter A. Distol
Steven Domeshek
Dean J. Donatelli, AIA
Lynn S. Dunham
Adel I. Elbas
Aurora Farewell
Michael J. Feeney
Jonathan A. Fine
Jeffrey A. Fleisher
Lorenzo Fletcher
Katherine Ford
Amy J.C. Forsyth
Robert A. Forwood
Scott Freidenrich
Katherine McDowell Frey
Matthew Funk
Christa J. Gaffigan
Joseph A. Gallagher, AIA
Kevin George
Jeffrey Gerhard
Michael J. Glynn
Dale E. Graff, AIA
Margaret Greco
Cheryl Grek
Barbara S. Griffin
Marilyn Grubb
Cristina A. Grummon
Andrew C. Guzik
Marion Haast
Carol Hahn
Michael Hanrahan
Mary L. Harris
John Hatch, AIA
Mary C. Hayden
Adam T. Hayes
Garrett W. Heher
Elizabeth B. Holah
Mary Horst
Gwen C. Huegel
Heidi A. Hughes
Marcus R. Hurley
Geraldine M. Jacobs
Natalie S. Jacobs
Anne James
Eduardo Jimenez

Judith L. Johnston
Christi A. Johnstone
Scott J. Kalner
Mohammad Ishtiaq Kamal
Jeffrey R. Kane
Maryann Kara-Jozwick
Robert F. Keppel
Zhanna Khodash
Philip L. Kianka, AIA
Michelle P. King
Melissa Kirsh
Jeanne S. Kisacky
Kurt L. Koevenig
Vicki L. Kohanek
Peter T. Kokoszka
Brian Kowalchuk, AIA
Walter M. Ksiazak
Heather L. Kubic
J. Ward Kuser
Jerry A. Laiserin, AIA
Tse-Chaing Leng
Ann Leopold
Brendon M. Levitt
Jan E. Lewis
John K. Lifland
Dennis G. Link
Dana Barry Lloyd
Susan E. Lockwood
James M. Mack
Darren J. Malone
Cecelia G. Manning
Dina Marinelli
Grace T. McAfee
John F. McDonald
Suzanne R. McGeorge
Sybil A. McKenna
Jasmine C. Meray-Spence
Oscar E. Mertz III
Daniel R. Millen, Jr., FAIA
Vincent A. Montrasio
Richard A. Mulder
Doris E. Muskett
Jennifer A. Myers
Marc R. Nemergut
Oliver Neumann
Mary E. Newman
Heli Ojamaa
Lisa Cruz Olcsvary
Sergey Olhovsky
John Orgren
Rosana E. Orlanski
Chad D. Owen
Pamela A. Parker
Harry J. Pell
Kristin Peterson Pennock
Andrea D. Perry
Robert A. Petito, Jr.
Grace Pierce
Emily C. Pierson
Helen K. Pinneo
Michael A. Plumeri
Bradford J. Prestbo
Laura L. Procaccino
Katherine Quigley
William A. Ranke
James L. Read
Sergio J. Reda
Ann F. Reed
Paul J. Repka

Cynthia M. Richter
John M. Roche
Marjorie Rothberg, AIA
Michael A. Runyon
Diego Samuel
Steven L. Schneider
Antonietta R. Schreiber
Quinn J. Schwenker
Catherine M. Seiwell
Catherine W. Sellers
James M. Seymore
Eran Siany
Victor J. Sittig
Martha Spangler-Anez
Jennifer L. Sparrow
Lynette Sroka, AIA
Theresa S. Sprayberry
Jennifer A. Stark, AIA
Neil Stempel
Brett J. Sterenson
Harper U. Stockham
Linda W. Strange
Arthur M. Sutherland
Christina Cowan Sym
Charles D. Tabick
Kathleen Tamasi
Michael E. Tartaglia, AIA
Andrew S. Thornton
William B. Uhl, AIA
Nicholas C. Upmeyer
Iowa Gay Uranga
Biju L. Vadakot
Debbie M. Vilar
Carolyn M. Wenczel
Mitchell White
Rob Whitlock, AIA
Lynda A. Widman
Timothy J. Williams
Mary M. Wilson
Gary H. Wolf
Scott C. Wolf
John M. Wriedt, AIA
Samuel A. Wykoff
Julie Yang
John K. Zeigler, Jr., AIA